CONFLICT OF INTERNATIONAL OBLIGATIONS AND STATE INTERESTS

CONFLICT OF INTERNATIONAL OBLIGATIONS AND STATE INTERESTS

by

Jung-Gun KIM
East Carolina University

and

John M. HOWELL
East Carolina University

MARTINUS NIJHOFF/THE HAGUE/1972

ISBN 978-94-015-0035-7 ISBN 978-94-015-0505-5 (eBook)
DOI 10.1007/978-94-015-0505-5

CONTENTS

PREFACE

This monograph is primarily addressed to the problem of avoidance, noncompliance or defiance of obligations related to international organizations by members and nonmembers. Structurally, it is a survey of the practices of uncooperative members and nonmembers set against a general statement of the norms of international organizations.

Minor disruptions in international affairs evoke conflicts of international obligations and state interests. Today, when the problems are grave and the prospects for peace are gloomy, there is an urgent need for scholars and practitioners of international relations to study and reflect upon the implications of prolonged disregard of international obligations during a time in which international organizations are increasing in numbers and in functions. To provide a systematic framework for this effort is a main purpose of this work.

Although the whole range of international organizations provide illustrations of these conflicts, practices within the United Nations system have been the focus of the study. There is no pretense of having made a comprehensive study of every international organization nor is there any claim that the coverage of cases having pertinence to the subject matter goes beyond the minimum required to illustrate these problems. From the many cases available, only those which promised to have most relevance or to provide the best understanding of the conflicts of international obligations and state interests were included.

Recognizing that readers may interpret their personal biases into these cases, the authors feel especially impelled to disavow a preference for the position of any particular state or the contending international organization. They have sought to present a reasonable perspective of the contemporary norms of international relations and to suggest the dangers of upsetting the balance between what international organizations can do and what states will not accept as obligations. If the approach has a "point of view" it is the gradualist philosophy that abrupt efforts by international organizations to increase their role and abrupt refusal by states to honor their obligations are detrimental to the orderly system that should be the goal of all international organizations and all states. In other words, it is assumed that the purposes and principles of the United Nations are and will remain desirable goals of the world community of states.

Although the authors have been colleagues for many years and have collaborated on all parts of this study, their separate interests have resulted in some division of labor. Jung-Gun Kim is primarily responsible for Chapters II, III, IX, and X. John M. Howell is primarily responsible for Chapters IV, V, VI, and VII. The remainder is a joint undertaking.

Jung-Gun Kim

John M. Howell

Greenville, North Carolina

CHAPTER I

AN OVERVIEW OF THE PROBLEM

States in the contemporary world have assumed greater international obligations than in the past, not only because areas of mutual concern and contacts among them have significantly increased during recent years but also because there has been an increase in the number of international organizations, both technical and political, which regulate international relations. This expansion of international obligations has been accompanied by efforts toward more effective international control of national affairs. Equally true is the observation that, as long as the basic unit of interplay in the international community remains the "sovereign" state, these units will be able to counter attempts to impose repugnant obligations upon them. Consequently, progress toward a more harmonious and united world, founded on the principles of peace and mutual security maintained by such international organizations as the United Nations, cannot be achieved unless there is a reasonable balance between the goals of individual states and those of international organizations.

During the life of the United Nations there has been a significant increase in the jurisdiction claimed by that organization, or at least a certain ascendancy in influence and prestige associated with its actions. For verification one need only consider the many incidents in which the United Nations has been involved or the trend to attach binding, legal obligations to General Assembly resolutions. Many matters, such as regulation of colonial areas, racial discrimination, and economic policies, which were once regarded within the domain of exclusive state control, have now become matters of international concern.

As more activities, issues and problems are claimed as the legitimate concern of international organizations, states have developed techniques for circumventing the consequent obligations. These efforts to maintain state discretion take many forms, ranging from mild resistance to harsh rejection, but for the purpose of simplification they have been classified here as: (1) avoidance, (2) noncompliance, and (3) defiance. As is usually the case with categories, this one has limitations. Because these techniques shade into each other and defy precise borderlines, they defy neat classification.

When faced with obnoxious, pending actions by international organizations, states initially resort to the technique of avoidance. Basically, this technique denies the existence of obligation or resorts to procedural technicalities to delay or to prevent the threatened issue from being considered or, if considered, from resulting in an international obligation.

As described here, techniques of avoidance are employed within the orderly operation of the international organ. The state seeking to avoid its obligation by this procedure presents a reasoned argument to the decision-making majority in the United Nations and presumably plans to accept the consequences if this tactic fails. Among the wide range of arguments that are available (other means of solution are in process; for practical reasons, international discussion would not advance the solution; a dispute or situation is too minor to come within the definitions of Chapter VI of the Charter), reservations within treaties establishing international obligations will be examined as a primary example of this technique.

By reservations, states attempt to take from international organs the power to deal with certain categories of matters at the time the organization is established. In essence, they are a preventive or prior means of avoiding obligations. From the state's point of view, an ideal reservation would foreclose any questioning before international organs of its conduct relating to the subject of the reservation. Failing the ideal, the state would expect the reservation to limit discussion to the preliminary question of the international organ's competence. As a last resort, the reservation would discourage a final recommendation for solution or result in an ineffectual stab toward resolution by the international organ. That reservations seldom live up to stated expectations will be illustrated at length in subsequent chapters.

Although of secondary importance, other means of avoidance have been tried sufficiently often to warrant a brief mention here as illustrations of the technique. A state wishing to avoid the pressure for compliance that may be generated within the United Nations may plead for dismissal by that body on the grounds that it is in the process of solution elsewhere, as for example in a regional organization or in bilateral negotiation. This argument was raised by the United States when the Cuban crisis was brought to the Security Council in 1960. When the Security Council began discussion of the charge that the Soviet Union was interfering in the internal affairs of Iran in 1946, the Soviet delegate insisted that the parties had entered into bilateral negotiations, that they should continue to resort to that method, and that the Council should not consider the complaint. Arguments that solutions should be sought outside the United Nations were fairly common in cases brought in the initial years of the United Nations.

During the debates regarding the Cyprus question in 1954 and 1955, the United Kingdom delegate argued that discussion would serve no useful purpose. Apparently this tactic met with temporary success, for, after a discussion largely devoted to practicalities, the plenary session dropped the item by a vote of fifty to none with eight abstentions. The United Kingdom delegate interpreted this course of events as support for his view that, for practical reasons, international discussion would not advance the resolution of the situation.

In response to the complaint in 1946 of Syria and Lebanon that French and British troops remained on their territory, the French delegate denied that the situation was of the nature referred to in Article 34 of the Charter (dispute or situation the continuance of which is likely to endanger the maintenance of international peace and security). He insisted that, if there was a dispute, the parties were required to negotiate it before calling on the United Nations.

When orderly processes of avoidance threaten to fail, states have emphasized their opposition within the processes of the organization by "walking out." The walkout technique is less effective as a means of indicating disapproval or claiming immunity from international obligations than it was in the immediate past. At present, the technique is apparently used not so much to reverse or otherwise to affect the decision of the substantive issue at hand, but more to indicate one's disapproval of the representatives (and of their country) and to cause diplomatic embarrassment or insult. Compare, for example, the walkout by the Union of South Africa in connection with the *Apartheid* case and the more recent, perhaps ceremonial, walkouts of the communist bloc nations when representatives of the Republic of China addressed the General Assembly.

Walkouts are utilized not only as a means to indicate disapproval and opposition to the pending decision but also to lay the groundwork for claiming at some later date that the issue was decided without the state's participation or that of all parties having interests in the issue. The latter could support the argument for injustice. In this use, however, the technique has shaded into the categories of noncompliance and defiance, for it becomes a reason for such action rather than a means for avoiding obligations.

Techniques of noncompliance operate outside the orderly processes of international organization and imply that its decisions are being overridden. On the most uncomplicated level these actions of noncompliance are not accompanied by great fanfare or openly-stated recalcitrance. The noncomplying state simply ignores the mandate of the international organ. In some instances, the act of noncompliance does not attract sufficient attention to make it a celebrated case. In others, the initial, simple noncompliance may be lost in a later more vocal and open defiance.

United Nations organs have passed a great many resolutions condemning the Union of South Africa for its racial policies and calling for a change in the situation, but South Africa has not responded. Neither has South Africa responded to United Nations requests that it withdraw its administration from Namibia. Several states have quietly failed to respond to General Assembly assessments to pay for peacekeeping operations. Others such as the Soviet Union have refused with some fanfare thereby shading their response toward the following category of defiance.

Failing in either or both of the above techniques, extremely disgruntled states may resort to various modes of defiance. Defiance, like noncompliance, is outside the orderly processes of international organization and is a category separate from noncompliance only in degree of rejection and the attitude of the recalcitrant state. Separate classification of the two serves more to recognize the distinction between the countless instances in which states ignore minor international obligations (which are acts of noncompliance) and the fewer very severe refusals to honor international obligations (which are acts of defiance seriously damaging international organizations).

Defiant states may take varied actions. They may announce refusal to honor decisions; they may resort to temporary dissociation from the organization (the case of Indonesian "intermezzo") or a partial break, (the case of French nonparticipation in NATO activities). The defiance may precede rather than follow international action, as in the case of Israel which forewarned, after the 1967 round of the Arab-Israeli war, that it would not be bound by any actions of the Security Council. Israel, however, did not completely dissociate itself from the United Nations.

Initiative for dissociation is not necessarily taken by states; the Organization of American States broke with the "present government" of

Cuba. Defiance may even be mutual as it was for a time in the case of the People's Republic of China and the United Nations, wherein refusal to seat representatives and defiance were reciprocal. Variations on these patterns will appear in subsequent case studies.

Each instance of avoidance, noncompliance or defiance, will reveal unique circumstances and varied underlying causes for the decision to ignore or otherwise defy the norms of the United Nations. For instance, the Israeli government gave as one reason for rejection of Security Council decisions the membership of that body. Israel has said that it does not and can not expect objective decisions from the Council since its composition (1969) is predominantly pro-Arab, if not anti-Israeli.

A different rationale appears in the case of the contest in Vietnam, involving a party which defies any solutions which are externally arrived at or imposed, including those under the auspices of the United Nations. As the North Vietnamese Government sees it, the war in Vietnam is a civil war in which no external entity has a right to interfere, in its conduct or in its ultimate solution. The so-called "Four Points" and "Five Points" programs of proposed methods of solution advanced by the North Vietnamese Government and by the National Liberation Front are illustrations of their insistence upon the principle of noninterference by external powers.

For a time, an even graver issue involved the People's Republic of China which defied the very essence of United Nations' involvement in Korea on the ground that United Nations actions in Korea was an American venture to exploit and expand its holdings in Asia. The People's Republic charged that United Nations action was nothing more than a cloak for American imperialism and as such, the decision on the Korean war manifested that the decision-makers in the United Nations are dupes of the colonial powers and their actions should be resisted and turned back.

Neither can one lose sight of the well-known Portuguese unwillingness (amounting to a defiance) to grant independence to its African colonies as directed by the Organization, on the ground that the territories were "overseas provinces" of Portugal not subject to the provisions of the Charter (specifically Article 73) regarding non-self-governing territories.

Nor, can one overlook the Soviet Union's refusal to pay certain expenses incidental to United Nations emergency operations, on the ground that these operations were based on illegal authority; namely upon the undertaking of the General Assembly to authorize enforcement measures when the Security Council is barred by a veto from making a decision. The Soviet Government maintained that, notwithstanding the advisory opinion of the International Court of Justice on the matter, the primary responsibility for the maintenance of international peace and security lies in the Council, not in the General Assembly, and the Council has neither recommended nor sanctioned the respective emergency operations. Hence the expense in question was regarded as in violation of the Charter, freeing member nations from the obligation to support the programs and to pay the expense associated with them. In related actions, many of the communist bloc nations "withdrew" from WHO and UNESCO in the mid 1950's because they disagreed with the respective organizations' goals and operations. Indonesia "withdrew" from the United Nations to demonstrate its extreme disapproval of the election of Malaysia to the Security Council in 1965. The list could be continued.

The problem of correctly labeling deviant activity of a state (whether it be avoidance, noncompliance or defiance) is complicated further by the fact that international norms change and states alter their response to obligations. Because the determination of avoidance, noncompliance, or defiance is basically over the question of intensity and scope of a deviant action, the standard which is employed to judge a given activity may change either because of the changes in the international standard itself or by the subsequent conformity by the deviant state, or both. The recent accommodation between the United Nations and the government of the People's Republic of China serves as a dramatic illustration of label-changing that resulted from concessions by the international organization and the state. The rising obligations of colonial powers after 1945, their initial recalcitrance, and their final acquiescence (with some exceptions of course) provide many other examples of the transient nature of any classification. Hence, so long as international politics provides the basis of international organization and so long as that basis is subject to change, determination of deviation from a given standard must always be understood in consideration of the specific time and circumstances.

In examining various attempts to deviate from the norms of international organizations, the authors have sought to indicate in each instance pertinent legal rules and practical effects of each problem. They have attempted to suggest the progressive stages (or sequence) of rejection of international obligations under the standard applicable or applied at that time.

Underlying all discussion of avoidance, noncompliance and defiance is the question of the extent of state obligation. The two following chapters assess international obligations of states. Most obligations result from membership in an organization, but obligations fall on nonmembers in some cases. Hence, a starting point must be an inquiry into the obligations to comply for member and nonmember states, both in legal and practical terms (Chapter II). This inquiry on the nature and general theory of obligations for member and nonmember states is followed by an examination of the validity of General Assembly resolutions, which have now become the principal instruments commanding observance or obedience to states. While it is true that certain actions under the Charter may be beyond the challenge of members (such as Security Council actions under Chapter VII of the Charter), not all actions under the auspices of the General Assembly are automatically binding. Yet, the General Assembly has become a center of United Nations actions, especially on matters of political and security questions. Hence, Chapter III examines the validity of General Assembly resolutions which often have been alleged as bases of international obligations.

Although only two chapters deal entirely with the question of international obligations, the subject is never completely absent from the remaining chapters. The expansion of international obligations is especially interwoven into the middle chapters which deal with the domestic jurisdiction reservation, for the history of the reservation is also an account of expanding international obligations of states. Chapter VI deals with effects of the Congo crisis on domestic life of a state. It also shows that such international activity may successfully override the opposition of a government that is scarcely viable.

Beginning with Chapter IV, the topics relate primarily to techniques of circumventing obligations. These techniques are arranged in a rough continuum, beginning with efforts at avoidance within the orderly processes of the organization and progressing to the most extreme defiance. Chapter IV examines some of the traditional modes of avoiding international obligations. The pleas of reservations, especially the claim of domestic jurisdiction, have been increasingly a topic of controversy, for their application can determine at an early stage the entire question of rights and wrongs of parties to a dispute. The question of reservations is unsettled, but the changing interpretation of these attempts to ward off international obligations in advance of their imposition is a key to understanding the system of orderly avoidance of international obligations.

Chapters V and VI, in turn, elaborate the cases leading to the failure of the domestic jurisdiction clause as a means of avoiding obligations and show the related attempts to increase the effectiveness of international endeavors to regulate the affairs of states. The ineffectiveness of reservations to protect state interests explains, in part, the progression to more recalcitrant devices. Chapter VII illustrates the transition to more defiant action by describing some of the efforts to avoid obligations when the customary domestic jurisdiction reservations fail.

The remaining chapters contain cases illustrating progressively recalcitrant actions of states. Beginning with the "mildest" (at least in reference to the present study) avoidance and noncompliance of United Nations obligations in the Middle East contest (Chapter VIII), on the one hand, to the other extreme of defiance in the Chinese case (Chapter X) on the other. The cases which fall in between (or otherwise provide contrasts from the two extremes) are included in Chapter IX. Although most chapters end with interim conclusions, the final chapter, Chapter XI, appraises the situation that faces the international community.

CHAPTER II

OBLIGATION OF COMPLIANCE FOR MEMBER AND NONMEMBER STATES UNDER THE UNITED NATIONS

MEMBER STATES

Article 103 of the Charter of the United Nations is emphatic in declaring that the obligations under the Charter shall take precedence over all other obligations which member nations have undertaken, or will have undertaken, and that all obligations contrary to the Charter principles shall not be entertained. Hence the superiority of the Charter as a law-making treaty accepted by virtually all states in the international community seems undeniable.

Accordingly, the Charter imposes certain obligations on its members such as: [1]

1. to fulfill all obligations of the Charter [Article 2 (2)];
2. to settle disputes through peaceful means [Article 2 (3-4)];
3. to assist the Organization (Articles 2, 5);
4. to meet financial obligations (Articles 17, 19);
5. to carry out the decisions of the Security Council (Articles 25, 48, 49);
6. to abide by enforcement action (Articles 43-45, 48);
7. to respect the provisions of the rights of self-defense (Article 51);
8. to inform the Security Council regarding any action taken under regional arrangements (Article 54);
9. to respect the provisions for economic and social cooperation (Article 56);
10. to respect the provisions for non-self-governing territories (Articles 73-74, 76, 84, 87, 88);
11. to respect the provisions for the Secretariat (Article 102);
12. to register all treaties (Article 102);

[1] For an authoritative elaboration of both general and specific obligations of membership in the United Nations, see Hans Kelsen, *The Law of the United Nations; A Critical Analysis of Its Fundamental Problems,* (New York; Frederick A. Praeger, 1966). pp. 87-110.

13. to grant legal status to organization, officials of members, officials of the organization (Articles 104-105);
14. to uphold obligations with respect to International Court of Justice (Article 94).

Generally speaking, actions counter to the Charter principles have the most immediate and grave impact when they involve international peace and security. In this connection, the Charter makes, again, certain emphatic claims: that unilateral use of or threat to use force by any state or states is prohibited,[2] as a matter of general principle, and that the exceptions to this general rule exist in only certain exceptional circumstances, namely (1) in conjunction with Article 51 of the Charter (in pursuance to the principle of "individual and collective self-defense") and (2) as enforcement measures under Chapter VII of the Charter.[3]

The record of defiance or noncompliance with the United Nations resolutions, in this regard, seems to indicate that at least part of the problem lies in the incapacity or inability of the organization definitively to decide or agree on the meaning of the various terms, such as "self-defense," "self-determination," and the like. This difficulty is in turn due to the incongruencies in the interpretation of the existence or lack of certain rights under (1) customary international law, (2) provisions of the Charter, and (3) circumstances of the actual case on hand.

The Charter seems to place the whole burden, or the right of interpretation, on the Security Council, which is empowered under Article 39 to determine "the existence of any threat to the peace, breach of the peace, or act of aggression ...." The finality of a Security Council

[2] Specifically, Article 2, par. 4 states: "All Members shall refrain in their international relations from the threat or use of force against the territorial integrity or political independence of any State, or in any other manner inconsistent with the Purposes of the United Nations." Article 2, par. 3 states further that member states are to "settle their international disputes by peaceful means in such a manner that international peace and security, and justice, are not endangered."

However, some writers would hold that the above-cited items in the Charter do not forbid the "threat or use of force" altogether nor unconditionally; rather that the prohibition is conditional upon (1) such usage being made "against the territorial integrity or political independence" of any state, and (2) otherwise making such usage inconsistent with the "Purposes of the United Nations." As for the purposes of the United Nations, it is noted that the stipulations of the purposes oulined in Article 1 do not import legal obligations to member states but are a declaratory statement of purpose. For this and related points, see Julius Stone, *Aggression and World Order*, (Berkeley: University of California Press, 1958), especially pp. 94-98.

[3] Some have added a third category (on the basis of Article 107 of the Charter) regarding actions taken against any state which during the Second World War has been an enemy of any signatory of the Charter.

decision on these matters is not to imply, of course, agreement within the Council over these issues. For instance, the Soviet bloc generally holds the strict view that the right of self-defense could be claimed only when and "if an armed attack occurs," hence, the gravity or immediacy of danger, size of forces involved, plus chronological considerations (e.g., who hit first) form the bases of determination. The Western bloc, however, seems to follow the somewhat flexible view that (1) since the reality of the contemporary international community is such as to prevent precise determination of an "armed attack," and (2) since states are susceptible to other forms of infringement upon their vital national interests, the determination of armed attack and ensuing rights stemming therefrom should be arrived at by an objective test of both a real attack and an imminent threat of attack in each case.[4]

Likewise, the principle of "self-determination" carries meanings which lack agreement. For instance, some authors, like S. K. Panter-Brick, attach certain sets of tests to validate the principle of "self-determination," such as "degree of finality with which the right to self-determination was exercised at the time of achieving independence," "the question of [geographic] size," and the like. Hence, if the size is below minimum and/or the political arrangement at the time of independence is accepted with finality, then, the entity (such as Biafra) might not legitimately claim the right of secession on the basis of "self-determination." This is, however, not to imply that the same or similar criteria would be valid for all cases.[5]

[4] For further discussion on the principle of "self-defense" and related points, see F. S. Lin, "Self-Defense—A Permissible Use of Force Under the U.N. Charter," *De Paul Law Review,* vol. 13 (1963), pp. 43-72; R. Higgins, "Legal Limits to the Use of Force by Sovereign States—United Nations Practice," *British Yearbook of International Law*, vol. 37 (1961), pp. 269-319; Kelsen, *op cit.,* pp. 791-805.

[5] Acknowledgedly, there is no universally agreed definition of the term "self-determination." The doctrine is allegedly associated with "the right of a group of people who consider themselves separate and distinct from others to determine for themselves the state in which they will live and the form of government it will have." However, such definition as this too must be regarded as a guide not as a definition. Assuredly, the concept is more a political than legal norm. While the concept has become a principal instrument through which many of the new states acquired their independence, especially since World War II, the concept was implicitly acknowledged in the (United States) Declaration of Independence, and saw its first international recognition in the form of President Woodrow Wilson's famous Fourteen Points (1918). For further discussion, see S. K. Panter-Brick, "The Right to Self-Determination: Its Application to Nigeria,"*International Affairs* (London), vol. 44,

Suffice it to say, on the basis of even a crude examination, that given the present status of the international community, and so long as there exists wide disagreement among members of the United Nations over particulars of Charter provisions, clear-cut and uniform application of the Charter norms appear unlikely.

Quite significantly, in the specific area of "international peace and security," the Security Council is empowered to determine the wrong (Article 39) and to prescribe the course of resolution—either provisionally (Article 40) or otherwise (Article 41), including use of armed forces (Article 42).

In this connection, two considerations of sanctions against members have to be clearly distinguished: (1) as an activity of a competent organ (i.e., the Security Council) involving determination of the wrong and prescription of remedial or corrective action, and (2) enforcement action involving actual and physical activities pursuant to the previously determined course.[6]

Professor Luard documents the activities falling in this category as follows: [7]

1. Calls on the parties to negotiate among themselves. [e.g., Kashmir-1952; West Irian-1955].
2. A special meeting of the General Assembly to consider the problem. [e.g., Palestine-1947/48; Suez-1956; Hungary-1956; Lebanon and Jordan-1958].
3. When fighting has already broken out, calls for a cease-fire have normally been made, usually by the Security Council. [e.g., Indonesia-1947; Arab-Israel-1948/49; Hungary-1956; Suez-1956; India-Pakistan-1965; Israel-Arab war-1967].
4. Commissions of inquiry or investigation, [e.g., regarding Korean unification-1947; Hungary-1957; apartheid in South Africa-1962].
5. Commissions whose function is mediation or conciliation rather than enquiry. [e.g., Indonesia-1947; Palestine-1947; Korea-1951; Indians in South Africa-1952; Kashmir-1958; the Congo-1960].

no. 2 (1968), pp. 254-266; Frederick L. Schuman, *International Politics,* (New York: Mc Graw-Hill Book Co., 1969), pp. 314-316; Jack C. Plano and Roy Olton, *The International Relations Dictionary,* (New York: Holt, Rinehart and Winston, Inc., 1969), pp. 121-122; Donald C. Blaisdell, *International Organization,* (New York: The Ronald Press, 1966), pp. 197-198.

[6] For a complete discussion on this point, see W. M. Reisman, "The Enforcement of International Judgments," *American Journal of International Law,* vol. 63, (1969), pp. 1-27. See also Blaine Sloan, "Implementation and Enforcement of Decisions of International Organizations," *Proceedings of the American Society of International Law,* 1968, p. 3.

[7] Evan Luard, *Conflict and Peace,* (Boston: Little, Brown and Co., 1968), pp. 333-334.

6. The appointment of one or more mediators. [e.g., Palestine-1948; Kashmir-1950; Cyprus-1964].
7. A representative of the Secretary-General may be appointed for private and informal consultations. [e.g., Thailand and Cambodia-1958; West Irian-1962; Buraimi-1963; Muscat-1965].
8. Dispatch of observers to the scene of hostilities. [e.g., Lebanon-1958; Yemen-1963/64].
9. A more permanent representative or "presence" may be established as an expression of concern and to exert a restraining influence. [e.g., Lebanon and Jordan-September 1958; Laos-1951; Cyprus-1964].
10. A visit by the Secretary-General himself. [e.g., Hungary-1956; South Africa-1961; Bizerta-1961; the Congo-1961].
11. Confidential negotiations under the auspices of the Secretary-General or President of the Assembly or Council. [e.g., Berlin blockade-1949; Chinese intervention in Korea-1950; Kashmir-1950, 1957; the nationalization of the Suez Canal-1956].
12. A technical commission to examine certain facts influencing a dispute and to make recommendations. [e.g., currency dispute in Berlin-1948].
13. A recommendation that the dispute be referred to the International Court of Justice. [e.g., Corfu Channel-1947].
14. The question may be left to a regional organization. [e.g., Costa Rica-Nicaragua-1948, 1955; Guatemala-1954; Honduras-Nicaragua-1957; Kuwait-1961; Cuba-1961; Panama-1964; Morocco-Algerian dispute-1963].

In view of the record cited above, it seems difficult to extract a rational relationship between enforcement actions and the gravity of dangers involved. Assuredly, therefore, legal determination and remedies of wrongs have given way, in the final analysis, to the politically determined, motivated, and enforced decisions which in almost all cases seem to be the most feasible compromise at the time. Because of this, meaningful insistence upon subscription to consistent legal norms based on the Charter has been sacrificed.

So long as expediencies of politically motivated decisions take precedence over objective, legally defined solutions, one must be prepared to accept the possibility of disgruntled members who would rather judge their own cases and denounce or ignore United Nations decisions.

In this connection, some writers observe that while the Security Council and the General Assembly were given broad powers to accomplish the objectives of the United Nations, these powers are, at least implicitly, not without limitations. Even if only by inference, the intention of the framers of the Organization to place certain limitations upon the United Nations itself is rather clear. Hence, Chapter I states that it is the purpose of the United Nations to "maintain international peace and security ...... [but to do so] ...... in conformity with the principle of justice and international law" [Article 1, (1)] and that "all Members shall settle their international disputes by peaceful means in such a manner that international peace and security, and justice, are not endangered" [Article 2, (3)].[8]

But, again, it cannot be forever maintained that international law (legal norms within the political dynamics of the international community) is unchanging and omnipotent, nor is it likely that states will necessarily abide by legal dictates, so long as legal norms are politically defined. Equally significant, the Charter does not place any priority upon legal settlement of disputes. In fact, if any priority may be inferred from the Charter, it is for a political mode of settlement (e.g. Article 39).

In the final analysis, therefore, so long as political expediencies dictate the course of United Nations action, political considerations will be likely to continue to dictate that certain states defy or ignore the decisions of the Organization, their membership obligations notwithstanding.

NONMEMBER STATES

Though not without precedent, The United Nations Charter declares emphatically that:

> The Organization shall ensure that states which are not Members of the United Nations act in accordance with [the principles of the United Nations Charter] so far as may be necessary for the maintenance of international peace and security. [Article 2, (6)]

This unilateral declaration for the assumption of jurisdiction by the Organization over the activities of nonmembers, though limited to the area of peace and security, has not been without controversy or disagreement.[9]

[8] For additional comments and elaborations, see Quincy Wright, *International Law and the United Nations,* (New York: Asia House, 1960), p. 43.

[9] For the specifics on the interpretation and analysis of Article 2 (6) of the Charter, see Richard A. Falk, "The Authority of the United Nations to Control Non-Members," *Rutgers Law Review,* vol. 19, no. 4 (1965), pp. 591-645. See also Leland M. Goodrich and Anne P. Simons, *The United Nations and Maintenance of International Peace and Security,* (Washington: Brookings Institution, 1955), pp. 128-143; Ruth B. Russell, *A History of the United Nations Charter, 1940-1945,* (Washington: Brookings Institution, 1958); A. Glenn Mower, Jr., "Observer Countries: Quasi Members of the United Nations," *International Organization,* vol. 20 (1966), pp. 266-283.

The League of Nations similarly claimed certain jurisdiction over nonmembers when their activities were directly related to the maintenance of international peace and security. Article 17 of the Covenant detailed the relationship by stating that:

1. In the event of a dispute between a Member of the League and a State which is not a Member of the League, or between States not Members of the League, the State or States not Members of the League shall be invited to accept the obligations of the League for the purposes of such dispute, upon such conditions as the Council may deem just. If such invitation is accepted, the provisions of Articles 12 to 16 inclusive shall be applied with such modifications as may be deemed necessary by the Council.
2. Upon such invitation being given, the Council shall immediately institute an inquiry into the circumstances of the dispute and recommend such action as may seem best and most effectual in the circumstances.
3. If a State so invited shall refuse to accept the obligations of membership in the League for the purposes of such dispute, and shall resort to war against a Member of the League, the provisions of Article 16 shall be applicable as against the State taking such action.
4. If both parties to the dispute when so invited refuse to accept the obligations of membership in the League for the purpose of such dispute, the Council may take such measures and make such recommendations as will prevent hostilities and will result in the settlement of the dispute.

Comparatively, the language of Article 2 (6) of the Charter is much more emphatic in claiming jurisdiction over nonmembers; the phrase used is "shall ensure" that nonmembers of the United Nations conform in their conduct to the norms of the Charter. Likewise, the Charter implicitly leaves no room for any nonmember state to defy or otherwise challenge the authority of the United Nations, at least when the problems of international peace and security are concerned.

Beyond this point, the general framework for the inclusion of nonmember states, if temporarily, within the respective system (United Nations or League) is quite similar. The Covenant envisions "invitation" as a mode of initial establishment of relationship with the nonmember state, although the "invitation" is conditioned by acceptance of "the obligations of the League for the purpose of . . . dispute, upon such conditions as the Council may deem just." The Charter includes participation by nonmembers generally within a similar framework. Article 32 of the Charter, in part, declares that "any state which is not a Member of the United Nations, if it is a party to a dispute under consideration by the Security Council, shall be invited to participate, without vote, in the discussion relating to the dispute. The Security Council shall lay down such conditions as it deems just for the participation of a state which is not a Member of the United Nations."

Additionally, although the Charter does not explicitly spell out the details as does Article 17 (2 - 4) of the Covenant, it appears reasonable to assume that if the Security Council determines (under Article 39) that a particular dispute which involves nonmembers or is between nonmembers is such as to constitute either "threat to the peace, breach of the peace, or act of aggression," then the dictates of Chapter VII will apply, hence, an analogy with Article 17 (2 - 4) of the Covenant.

Some differences between the two systems are equally apparent. For one, the Covenant seems to leave no privilege of bringing the dispute by nonmembers to the Council for settlement,[10] whereas the Charter allows such privileges to nonmembers [Article 35, (2)]; for another, the Covenant leaves for nonmembers the possibility of defying the League. For instance, under the dictates of Article 17 of the Covenant, nonmembers may be involved in the League system by invitation, provided that the nonmember state is a party to an international dispute and only if disputant nonmembers accept the invitations with "such conditions as the Council" might place. Article 2 (6) and Article 32 of the Charter seem to imply that assumption of jurisdiction by the United Nations over a nonmember disputant is mandatory, and that, presumably, no dispute which is deemed as being either "threat to the peace, breach of the peace, or act of aggression," whoever may be the disputants, may be ignored by the United Nations.

Additionally, while both documents speak of "state(s)" which are not members of the respective international organization (an invited entity is implicitly recognized as a "state"), the Charter system allows flexibility: The Provisional Rules of Procedure of the Security Council state (Rule 39) that "The Security Council may invite members of the Secretariat or other persons, whom it considers competent for the purpose, to supply it with information or to give other assistance in examining matters within its competence."[11]

The League seldom used Article 17; the only significant case that involved a nonmember state of the League was the *Eastern Carelia* case (involving a nonmember government, Russia, and a member government,

[10] Possibly it may be inferred that Article 17 (1) might be interpreted to allow nonmember's utilization of the League. But this point seems not at all certain, insofar as the writer can ascertain.

[11] Goodrich and Simons, *op. cit.*, pp. 130-131.

Finland) in which the Russian government's refusal to take part in any League procedure of settlement was generally left unanswered by the League.[12] In contrast and in the case of the United Nations, though it may be an exception rather than a rule, the Korean war symbolized the role of the United Nations in regard to nonmembers. It must be recalled that neither of the disputing governments in Korea, nor the People's Republic of China, was then a member of the United Nations. One recalls also the *Corfu Channel* case, in which one of the disputants (Albania) was then not a member of the United Nations, yet the United Nations was very much involved in the case.

In short, the Charter system seems to envision a reciprocal agreement in which unilateral declaration of the assumption of jurisdiction over a nonmember party to a dispute is reciprocated by the privilege of any state or entity (Article 32 and Rule 39) involved in a dispute to utilize the Organization's machinery, provided that "conditions" laid down by the Security Council are accepted. Often, the Council does not specify the Article in the Charter in order, presumably, to avoid any inference to the invitee's being a "state" or placing "conditions" (i.e., the invitation extended to the People's Republic of China in 1950).

The controversy regarding legal validity of an international organization to claim jurisdiction over nonmembers has been varied and lengthy. In its broad generality, those who support the validity [e.g., Article 2, (6)] of the United Nations to assume unilateral jurisdiction over nonmembers seem to base their view upon the idea of what is commonly referred to as "functional necessity." This theory holds that unless it is the Organization's right to command nonmembers to conform to and restrain their conduct in accordance with the basic precepts of the Charter (at least in the basic sphere of international peace and security), the foundation of the organization is made meaningless; hence, the general good of the international community (that of peace and security) demands that nonmembers too must be made to conform to the Charter norms insofar as their conduct relates to the maintenance of international peace and security.

On the other hand, those who question the validity of the United Nation's authority to assume jurisdiction over nonmembers tend to follow

[12] It is to be noted that the Council took notice of the *case* on September 27, 1923, and passed a resolution stating that it could take action if the circumstances should make action necessary in the interest of peace. In general, however, an overall unwillingness or inability of the League to act against the nonmember (Russia) appears as a valid analysis in the present context.

the rather rigid norms of traditional international law, in particular, laws governing treaties. In essence, this school holds that the Charter of the United Nations is a multilateral treaty, having validity limited to its signatories and others acceding to the treaty. Therefore, it cannot bind nonsignatories whatever may be claimed unilaterally, for to do so would be a violation of the basic precepts of international law, which in the final analysis is based on the sovereignty of states.

On the whole and in general, it appears that apart from the general issue of the competency of an international organization to "legislate" on behalf of nonmembers, the power claimed in Article 2 (6) (that is, the authority of the United Nations to claim jurisdiction over nonmembers in the limited area of international peace and security) seems an accepted principle, perhaps not so much because of its consistency with the traditional norms of international law, but due to consideration of the practicalities of the problems of war and peace and in view of the fact that there have not been any really serious challenges to the principle.

CONCLUSION

In the final analysis, the main difference between the actions of member states and nonmember states against principles of the United Nations is a matter of determining whether or not a given action falls, or does not fall, within the confines of Article 2 (6) of the Charter, which in the most immediate sense is to say whether or not the Security Council (perhaps General Assembly as well) determines that a particular activity of a nonmember state constitutes "a threat to the peace, breach of the peace or act of aggression." Should the Council decide that any activities of a nonmember fall within the purview of Article 2 (6), sanctions which may be imposed by the Organization seem to differ very little, if any, between member and nonmember states.

In this connection, the issue of prime and practical importance appears to be not only that of Article 2 (6) but also of Article 2 (7). Although application of enforcement measures under Chapter VII of the Charter are unaffected by Article 2 (7), this article does necessitate the determination of the circumstances and activities which are properly of "international concern," and provides the greatest single claim of immunity from international intervention upon "matters which are essentially within the domestic jurisdiction."[13]

[13] See the succeeding discussion in Chapter IV, V, and VI.

CHAPTER III

VALIDITY OF THE GENERAL ASSEMBLY RESOLUTIONS; AN INQUIRY

INTRODUCTION

There is considerable difference in the opinions expressed as to how binding United Nations resolutions are or should be.

To begin with, the point of central importance appears to be the establishment of the relationship between the Charter and international law. If the Charter is or ought to be considered as a part of that body of legal norms enforceable in international tribunals, it seems difficult to deny that certain activities of the United Nations which are undertaken in pursuance to, or are demanded by, the Charter create legal obligations for its members. Additionally, most writers and practitioners in international relations seem to agree that the Charter, as a multilateral treaty, does create certain rights and obligations toward its members and is therefore a binding legal instrument.

However, apart from this general agreement as a matter of principle disagreements do exist when specifics of certain aspects or activities under the Charter are involved. In general, the disagreements over the binding nature of certain aspects of the Charter, or certain activities undertaken by an organ created by the Charter, are seemingly centered around several related considerations: (1) lack of an authoritative interpreter of the Charter; (2) difficulty in precisely assessing certain actions of the Organization within the traditional norms of international law; (3) the problem (or test) of enforcability. A brief examination of each of these points will be presented with emphasis on the significance of United Nations resolutions.[1]

[1] For a more comprehensive study on this and related points, see Alex C. Castles, "Legal Status of U.N. Resolutions," *Adelaide Law Review*, vol. 3 (1967), pp. 68-83; Obed Asamoah, "The Legal Effect of Resolutions of the General Assembly,"

LACK OF AN AUTHORITATIVE INTERPRETER OF THE CHARTER

The following are some of the important reasons for the difficulty in interpreting the Charter : (1) certain inherent and seemingly contradictory principles in the document; (2) what some writers (Quincy Wright, for example) call "insusceptibility for interpretation" under traditional norms of international law; (3) priority of political decisions, sometimes demanded by the Charter; and (4) the ineffective role of the International Court of Justice.

Contrddictory Principles

Even a cursory glance at the Charter reveals that certain of its principles are seemingly contradictory if not self-negating. For instance, the so-called "sovereign equality" as the basis of the organization as declared in Article 2 (1) is negated by the composition of the Security Council (namely, positions accorded to its permanent members) and the obligation of all United Nations members to abide by its decisions. Similarly, while Articles 10, 11, and 12, Chapters VI and VII, and Article 62 and 73 seem generally to empower the United Nations without any meaningful limitations upon its prerogatives, Article 2 (7) negates them by declaring that "nothing in the present Charter shall authorize the United Nations to intervene in matters which are essentially within the domestic jurisdiction of any state" although, acknowledgedly, the stipulation of Chapter VII is excluded.[2]

In the same vein, the rights of "individual and collective self-defense" granted under Article 51 seem to be negated by the declaration of Article 53 (1) which specifically condemns enforcement action taken without the consent of the Security Council. What is important in this

Columbia Journal of Transnational Law, vol. 3 (1965), pp. 210-230; Babriella R. Lande, "The Changing Effectiveness of General Assembly Resolutions," *The United Nations,* Richard A. Falk and Saul H. Mendlovitz, ed., (New York: World Law Fund, 1966), pp. 227-237.

[2] Evan Luard, *Conflict and Peace,* (Boston: Little, Brown and Co., 1968), p. 284. For a more technical study of the question of "domestic jurisdiction," see John M. Howell, "Domestic Questions in International Law," *Proceeding of the American Society of International Law,* 1954, pp. 90-99, and "Delimiting 'Domestic Jurisdiction'," *Western Political Quarterly,* vol. 10, (1957), pp. 512-526, by the same author.

connection is not the specifics of the above-cited, but the recognition of possibly contradictory principles in the Charter which make it subject to dissimilar interpretations. And so long as there are, therefore, principles which tend to support dissimilar standards, though based on the same document, it is only understandable that states' claims to legality over a given action will be justified through careful, discriminatory and selective reliance on that portion of the Charter which supports their actions, irrespective of consistency with the general purposes and principles of the Charter.

Difficulty of Legal Assessment under Traditional International Law

While the degree of preciseness of the language used in the Charter is not in and of itself necessarily a point of shortcoming (consider for instance, the Constitution of the United States and the development of its government), inherent ambiguities do often create room for disagreement over the precise meaning.

For instance, while the foundation of the United Nations system is acknowledgedly based on the effective operation of the collective security system, many of the essential terms and concepts are left undefined, such as "intervene," "situation," "party to a dispute," "regional arrangement," "self-defense," and others.

In addition, the "hortatory nature" of the various principles often prevents, or at minimum makes difficult, a normal juridical determination of the precise meaning or application. This difficulty, coupled with the merely advisory role of the Court, makes the Charter less than susceptible to the traditional subject of juridical analogy. One had to only compare and reflect upon the various new members which had been admitted during the recent year. While it is admittedly ill-advised, if not dangerous, to suggest that any of these states fail to meet the basic conditions outlined in Article 4, it is true that these new states meet the requirements of Article 4 only because they were so voted by the collectivity of the membership based on political expediencies of their individual state's national interests, which may or may not indeed meet the original and desired intent of the framers of the Charter. Similarly, the United Nations' record of intervention and handling of disputes reveal dissimilar standards.

Again, so long as political expediencies are preconditions for the determination of key concepts of the collective security system, it is only understandable that the dynamics of international politics make it impossible to expect consistent, uniform, and juridical prescription of the characteristics of each term or concept employed in the Charter. This is, however, not to minimize the significance of international organizations as "law-making" agencies.[3]

Shortcomings here discussed are also related to the point immediately following.

Priority of Political Decisions

It seems undeniable, as one author finds, that:

> ... most interpretations of the Charter leading to development of the United Nations system have been made politically by political organs rather than juridically by the International Court ... Political interpretation has enabled the organization on many occasions to free itself from its own rules and limitations and has often permitted action when strict legal interpretation would have foreclosed or hobbled it.[4]

Similarly, the Charter at times *demands* that certain decisions ought to be arrived at by political organs exclusively and implicitly based on political considerations only. Hence, and as a classic case, the Security Council's exclusive right to "determine the existence of any threat to the peace, breach of the peace, or act of agression" (Article 39) is beyond the challenge of any organ, including the Court, nor can any organ, within or without the United Nations system, challenge the independence of the Security Council in this regard. Therefore, it appears that "where provisions are interpreted in the light of aims and principles or when they are hortatory in their content, as in Chapter XI of the Charter and to some extent in Chapter XII, political judgment seems to be required

[3] In this connection, the following might suggest some of the significant thoughts on the problem of General Assembly resolutions: Samuel A. Bleicher, "The Legal Significance of Re-citation of General Assembly Resolutions" *American Journal of International Law,* vol. 63 (1969), pp. 444-478; D.H.N. Johnson, "The Effect of Resolutions of the General Assembly of the United Nations," *British Yearbook of International Law,* vol. 32 (1955-56), pp. 97-122; O. Schachter, "The Quasi-Judicial Role of the Security Council and the General Assembly," *American Journal of International Law,* vol. 58 (1964), pp. 960-965; F. Blaine Sloan, "The Binding Force of a Recommendation of the General Assembly of the United Nations," *British Yearbook of International Law,* vol. 25 (1948), pp. 1-33.

[4] Jack C. Plano and Robert E. Riggs, *Forging World Order,* (New York: MacMillan Co., 1967), p. 55.

by the Charter itself to determine...the meaning to be ascribed to these provisions." [5]

On the other hand, the hortatory nature of certain portions of the Charter, coupled with political determination of the Charter standards, sometimes leads to unfortunate, confusing and irregular criteria depending upon the particulars of the parties and circumstances involved. Furthermore, these shortcomings sometimes cause the aggrieved party, which is or has been a subject of United Nations action, to claim immunity from the United Nations decisions by charging either (1) that the decisions are not "in accordance with the....Charter," or (2) that the decisions are in violation of international law—i.e., the concept of domestic jurisdiction—or both. In either case, if the charge is entertained, freedom of action for the state is given some basis in law.

This possibility, indeed a reality, is doubly significant and immediate in view of the fact that the International Court of Justice lacks the power to render binding and final decisions on matters pertaining to certain fundamental concepts outlined in the Charter. Indeed, irrespective of the United Nations claims to the contrary, the Rhodesian government among others has been relying on this precise argument to disclaim its obligation to abide by United Nations decisions (for further discussion on the Rhodesian question, see Chapter V).

Considering that the line separating areas of domestic jurisdiction and that of "international concern" is at best fluid and is seemingly devoid of immediate and precise definition, the contest between (1) actions of international organizations to "internationalize" various issues and endeavors in the name of international peace and security, and (2) the counter claims of states aimed to negate their obligations so construed will likely continue and may result in further avoidance, noncompliance, or defiance on the part of states. This likelihood is especially great when and if the matter in dispute concerns "vital interests" or other immediate political or security interests of the states.

Notwithstanding Article 39, the *Uniting for Peace Resolution* empowers the General Assembly to make "appropriate recommendations to

[5] Castles, *op. cit.,* p. 80. For a discussion on this and related points, see Quincy Wright, *International Law and the United Nations,* (New York: Asia House, 1960), p. 43. Professor Wright finds that the priority of political over legal considerations is fundamental to the Charter of the United Nations. While legal considerations should form a foundation of the United Nations actions, he infers that the framers of the Charter had placed preference for political determination and secondarily for its legal consistency.

Members for collective measures, including in the case of a breach of the peace or act of aggression the use of armed forces when necessary, to maintain or restore international peace and security." Powers stipulated in the resolution become operative only if the Council fails to "exercise its primary responsibility for the maintenance of international peace and security" due to the "lack of unanimity of the permanent members," but, in any event, Articles 10 and 11 of the Charter empower the General Assembly to "discuss any questions or any matter within the scope of the Charter or relating to the powers and functions of any organs provided for" and to consider the general principles of cooperation in the maintenance of international peace and security...."

Because the General Assembly has become a focal point of practical importance during recent years insofar as being able to declare a situation to be a threat to the peace and being able to command the support of the greatest possible number of states, special weight must be attached, it seems, to its recommendations or actions.

In short, the Charter, perhaps wisely, left determinations of certain questions to the political organs, including the authority of each organ to interpret its competence. Again, this does not facilitate consistent or juridical determination of the intent, meaning, competence, and required action of the Charter.

Ineffectiveness of the International Court of Justice

Bases of the relatively weak role of the Court in this context stem from (1) the Article 95 proviso that differences may be submitted to tribunals other than the Court; (2) the limitation of the Court's decision, namely the nonbinding nature of the Court's findings to the organs of the United Nations; (3) the unwillingness, at least thus far, of the members of the United Nations to submit their disputes to the Court.

Perhaps most well-known, and in some way illustrative of this point, is the case of *Certain Expenses of the United Nations* [6] wherein the Court, by a nine to five majority, decided that "the expenses relating to the U.N.E.F. and O.N.U.C. forces were 'expenses of the organization' within Article 17 (2) of the Charter." Despite the therefore seemingly legal nature of the assessment involved, the General Assembly saw fit not to enforce the otherwise enforceable finding of the Court.

So long as the ideals of judicial settlement do not play a significant role in international relations in resolving disputes, and so long as states

[6] I.C.J. Rep. (1962) p. 151.

are reluctant to accept, or are opposed to, the idea of the compulsory adjudicatory role of the Court, and so long as the role of the Court is limited to an "advisory" function, it seems difficult to expect clear and definitive juridical interpretations of the Charter.

This inability, however, to establish decisions and interpretations of the Charter juridically arrived at must be considered in the light of the advantages and disadvantages inherent in the politically derived interpretations.

Admittedly, and on the positive side, politically motivated and derived interpretations of the Charter will allow flexibility nominally unavailable in the juridically derived interpretation; the actions undertaken under the auspices of the *Uniting for Peace Resolution* as an alternative to action sponsored by the Security Council is an example in point.

Furthermore, political interpretations, by their very nature tend to encourage compromise and a negotiated course of action which are of far more practical importance than a juridically derived decision in which a retreat is either impossible or far more costly to a state.

On the negative side, politically derived interpretations tend to produce, in the course of time, growing uncertainty as to the exact meaning of the Charter and contain the potential to produce chaos in international standards.

In short, so long as a meaningful agreement in the international community relationship between international law and certain actions arising under the Charter of the United Nations is not immediately forthcoming, it will be difficult to establish with precision any meaningful juridical determination of United Nations actions (other than in a few exceptional cases where such determination is obvious, e.g., actions under Chapter VII of the Charter).

DIFFICULTY IN PRECISELY ASSESSING CERTAIN ACTIONS OF THE ORGANIZATION WITHIN THE TRADITIONAL NORMS OF INTERNATIONAL LAW

The second broad area of importance in the consideration of legality of United Nations resolutions under international law is the obvious difficulty of precisely assessing certain actions of the United Nations within the norms of traditional international law. Basically, this point revolves around whether or not resolutions of the United Nations are (or are not) "laws" (international law).

It must be acknowledged from the outset that there is no disagreement over the competency of the Security Council to undertake decisions, especially on matters coming under the purview of Chapter VII (and in certain instances, Chapter VI). Hence, the discussion of the legally binding nature of United Nations resolutions centers around the General Assembly actions.

Most of the arguments advanced in support of the binding nature of United Nations resolutions seem to be based on, among others, the following points: (1) the proper terminology used in resolutions is irrelevant; (2) "obligation" and "effect" are not synonymous and the lack of "effect" does not eliminate legal "obligation" of resolutions; (3) traditional norms of international society—international law—are and have been largely European oriented, hence immune from the claims of global consensus, but United Nations resolutions are more a reflection of the contemporary universal norms; (4) resolutions of the United Nations are binding, at least to all its members [and, when issues of international peace and security are involved, to nonmembers, as well under Article 2 (6)] because they are an "elaboration of obligations already assumed by members" as signatories to the Charter or by virtue of accession to it in case of admitted members; (5) certain resolutions, such as those relating to budget, are in fact "decisions" binding upon members without their consent; (6) certain courts gave support and made decisions on the basis of United Nations resolutions.[7]

First, it is observed that the proper terminology attached to particular actions of the organs of the United Nations is of no significant consideration in the test of the binding nature of United Nations resolutions; the truer test is the determination, explicitly stated or implied, of the intent of the resolutions. Additionally, certain resolutions of the General Assembly (for instance, dealing with inferior organs, admission of new members, and the like) are in fact binding decisions, although the decision is stated in a "resolution" form.[8] On the other hand, there are,

[7] In this connection, see Asamoah, *op. cit.,* especially pp. 226-227. See also Rzysztof Skubiszewski, "The General Assembly of the U.N. and its Power to influence National Action," *Proceedings of the American Society of International Law,* 1964, pp. 153-161.

[8] On the whole, and in general, decisions under this category belong to internal workings of the organs concerned and do not, at least immediately, affect the "ordering" of the international community. Some of the illustrations of this category are resolutions which:

1. appoint Secretary-General;

acknowledgedly, resolutions which do not have the force of "binding" arrangements.

Second, while "laws" usually create "obligation" and hence the "effect," the lack of "effect" is in and of itself not the absolute requirement of a "law". As an illustration, it is argued that not all "obligations" result in "effect" (in the sense of implementation) nor are all acts that are "implemented" necessarily legal or under legal obligation; what is legal may not be implemented, and what is implemented may not be legal. In any event, resolutions of the United Nations, it is alleged, do create "obligations," and to that extent, and in that sense, they are "laws" even in the absence of the implementation. This is especially so when resolutions call for specific discharge or restraint of certain functions or when there is an accumulation of resolutions on the same or similar subject, or when a resolution is supported by the majority or even unanimity of the member nations.

Third, notwithstanding their seemingly irregular, if not contradictory, stand on the issue, Afro-Asian states in particular have demanded that inasmuch as there is no "international" law in the sense of the universal moral and legal code, and inasmuch as traditional international law is born and nurtured in the European civilization which has not always been "just" nor "moral," the only practicable substitute for international norms, even temporarily, will have to be the resolutions of the United Nations, which at least express a consensus that is as near to universal as is practicable. Hence, they will have to be regarded as binding contemporary norms of international relations.

Fourth, the idea that resolutions are mere elaborations of the obligations already assumed as conditions of membership presumes that the

2. determine the Rules of Procedure (of either the Security Council or the General Assembly);
3. admit, suspend, or expel members;
4. approve and apportion budget;
5. elect non-permanent members of the Security Council; other members to ECOSOC, non-administering state portion of Trusteeship Council membership; members to their subsidiary bodies;
6. approve international agreements, such as agreements between UN and specialized agencies, or
7. appoint members of ICJ.

In all cases mentioned above (there may be more), the binding nature of actions within the respective organs (whether the General Assembly or the Security Council makes them) is indisputable.

Charter is a multilateral treaty creating legal obligations of observation in "good faith" and that fundamental questions of legality have to be considered in relation to actions which are necessary to implement the intent of the Charter. And since the Charter is a multilateral treaty, actions undertaken in its pursuance, so long as they are not contradictory to its basic principles, are also legal.

Fifth, as stated previously, and as will be discussed later, certain actions of the General Assembly are complete as an act of law. While this area is largely confined to internal operation of the Organization, budgetary matters, matters pertaining to election of members to other organs of the United Nations, and the like are seemingly decisions of a binding nature. Hence, resolutions do create and define obligations and effect.

The final argument, not that this is an exhaustive list, involves certain instances wherein courts and national governments gave meaning and weight to United Nations resolutions—as a proof of the "law". As, for instance, in the *Corfu Channel* case, the International Court of Justice interpreted the Special Agreement (entered into between the two parties and which had been "drawn up as a result of the Security Council resolution of April 9, 1947") "in the light" and for the purpose of giving "full effect" to the resolution.[9]

Similarly, the Guatemalan government placed heavy emphasis on the resolution of the General Assembly dealing with the permanent sovereignty of states over their natural wealth and resources in support of their unilateral seizure of foreign properties in 1952.[10]

Likewise, the United States Supreme Court heard pleas of the Justice Department which were based on resolutions of the various international organizations.

From the foregoing, it seems apparent that while the merits of each argument might vary, certain norms approaching "law" in a very general sense seem undeniable. As stated previously, there are, also, those who believe that, while resolutions of the United Nations do acknowledgedly provide "moral force" and accompanying "moral obligations," they are not and cannot be construed as being a full act of "law." Those who argue inadmissibility (in varying degrees) of General Assembly resolutions as creating legal obligations seem to base their positions on the following grounds.

[9] See Asamoah, *op. cit.*, pp. 226-227; Skubiszewski, *op. cit.*, pp. 156-161.
[10] *Ibid.*

First, international law is to be found either in "treaties, practices of states, judicial decisions, or decisions of other tribunal authorized to declare law," and inasmuch as resolutions of the United Nations are none of the above stated, they are not and cannot be laws, or otherwise create legally binding obligations.

Second, while conceding broad powers of the General Assembly, under Articles 10-14, to deal with various aspects of the United Nations or of any of the organs created by the Charter, it is noted that this power is limited to the power to "discuss" and to "recommend," and that while, again recommendations create moral obligations to its member to give "due consideration in good faith," they do not and cannot create binding legal obligations. Hence, and notwithstanding the validity of a binding force in certain matters pertaining to its internal operations, General Assembly resolutions cannot establish, alter, or terminate the "ordering of international community."

Third, some of the leading jurists, though not without disagreement, acknowledge that General Assembly resolutions create no binding legal obligations, although states are morally obligated to give "due consideration in good faith" to a resolution, as stated by Judge Lauterpacht in the *Voting Procedure* case.[11] Both Hans Kelsen and Sloan (to name two) are in agreement with this proposition.

Fourth, in the absence of Security Council action under Chapter VII of the Charter, General Assembly resolutions conflict with Article 2 (7) of the Charter wherein the latter has been sanctified in the history of international law. The Union of South Africa relied basically on this thesis to support its unwillingness to be bound by the resolution dealing with *apartheid.* A similar stand was taken by Australia when United Nations resolutions challenged the validity of the union between Papua and New Guinea.[12] It must be acknowledged that, in the absence of a clearcut definition on the limits of domestic and international jurisdiction, claims of this type are perhaps not surprising.

Finally, and notwithstanding the *Uniting for Peace Resolutions,* it is alleged that unless members of the United Nations (acting as signatories to a treaty) agree to the intent and language of a resolution creating legal obligation, no resolution of the General Assembly, however construed, can be regarded as legally binding, since the organ does not on its own right have the power to undertake "decisions".

[11] I.C.J. Rep. (1955), p. 120.

[12] Castles, *op. cit.*, pp. 76-77.

In the final analysis, it appears that the two exceptions—seemingly acknowledged by all—are that: (1) on certain matters (chiefly falling within the internal organization and operation of the United Nations) resolutions can create binding obligations, such as the decisions of budgetary matters, but on all other matters which demand actions relating to "ordering of international community," the General Assembly lacks power to undertake binding decisions [13] and (2) the Security Council can make binding decisions, especially under Chapter VII (and Chapter VI as well in certain instances).

[13] Admittedly, this is a controversial point. It appears, however, that difference of opinion amongst the scholars on this point is a matter of degree and of what constitutes the "ordering of international community." In this connection, see also, Leslie Knox Munro, "Recent Developments in the Role of the General Assembly in the Maintenance of Peace," *Proceedings of the American Society of International Law,* 1958, pp. 34-47.

CHAPTER IV

RESERVATIONS AS DEVICES FOR AVOIDING INTERNATIONAL OBLIGATIONS

INTRODUCTION

While states have multiplied their general obligations by joining international organizations, they have concurrently devised reservations to escape regulation in specific cases that may arise subsequently. The practice of giving with one hand while taking with the other has fostered extended jurisdictional debates, but these precautions that have been taken to avoid obligations and this resort to legal arguments have been generally unsuccessful. Although the pleas for state discretion have usually been expertly presented, they have been based on norms that have been replaced by new international norms or overridden (as have property rights in the face of personal liberties) by an expanded international organization membership which has reordered the hierarchy of international values. One may dislike this course of events, but this does not change the fact that world opinion expressed in a vote in an international organization carries considerable weight.

The concept of a "reserved domain" against international interference naturally accompanied movements toward permanent international organization. States were not willing to accept blanket obligations without protecting themselves against the unknown future. The various reservations they devised to accomplish this protection had in common one characteristic; they aimed to diminish the general obligations that were accepted by membership.[1] Even the most cynical members of the world community, as well as the most forthright, offer reasons when they seek to avoid membership obligations, and they have naturally made use of available reservations. The effort here will be confined to an assessment

[1] Similar reservations are also included to diminish the effects of treaties not related to international organizations, but they are not dealt with here.

of only two reservations that have been drafted to protect states from the membership obligations of international organization. By far the more significant is the domestic jurisdiction clause in Article 2 (7) of the Charter of the United Nations. The other is the particular category of "prior disputes" reservations that deals with the issues arising from the peace settlement of the Second World War (Article 107 of the Charter).

Reservations may appear in the body of an agreement and at the end of the negotiations. The most common use of the term "reservation" refers to a declaration by a state when signing, ratifying and acceding to an agreement by which it specifies certain limits to the effect of the agreements. These reservations to treaties constitute a "motley group" [2] which have been of more legal interest because of the technical problems they raise in connection with the applicability of multilateral conventions between two reserving states (or between reserving states and states not reserving) than for their effect on the general scope of international obligations set forth in the treaty. Furthermore, they have been relatively insignificant in treaties establishing international organizations, for, as is well known, such reservations to the United Nations Charter were not allowed.

Reservations within the constitutive documents of international organizations have been relatively ineffective, not so much because their applicability was put in doubt by the possibility that mutual consent to them was lacking but because of an unwillingness on the part of the decision-making majority to be bound by them.

Perhaps it should be emphasized that, in their usual form, reservations are devices for an orderly avoidance of international obligations. Their purpose is to bar the international organization from imposing an obligation on a state by establishing the organization's incompetence to do so; they are preventive. Their position and statement implies that they will apply only through the established processes of the organization. That is, a state makes its plea and, if it is found to be invalid, the state accepts the consequences or the obligations that may result.

A variation of the domestic jurisdiction reservation that has appeared primarily in acceptances of the compulsory jurisdiction of the International Court of Justice, the so-called Connally-type reservation, attempts to give the reserving state the authority to determine the effect

[2] For an excellent study of this category see William W. Bishop, Jr., "Reservations to Treaties," *Recueil des Cours,* vol. 103 (1961), pp. 255-260.

of the reservation.[3] This self-serving reservation will be mentioned briefly in a later chapter as a transitional stage between the attempts to employ reservations as a device to avoid obligations while remaining obedient to the international organization and defiance of the obligation that arises after the attempt fails to bar international jurisdiction to impose the obligation. The remainder of the present chapter will deal briefly with Article 107 of the Charter and in more detail with the rise and decline of the domestic jurisdiction reservation as devices to avoid international obligations. The following chapter will summarize leading cases in this cycle of the domestic jurisdiction concept.

THE RESERVATION IN ARTICLE 107 OF THE CHARTER

Article 107 of the Charter falls into the category of reservations common in treaties of pacific settlement called "prior disputes." When they are applicable and acceptable in a case, prior disputes reservations may be very effective. Two such reservations blocked settlement in the *Phosphates in Morrocco* case [4] and the *Iranian Oil Company* case.[5]

Three distinct categories are commonly included under the heading of "prior disputes." The most common reservation refers to disputes that may arise out of events or situations prior to the date of the treaty. A second category prohibits the reopening, under the provisions of the new treaty, of disputes that had already been settled between the parties prior to the date of the treaty. A narrower category than either of the foregoing reserves something specific in the past, such as disputes arising out of a past war.

The occurrence of reservations to disputes arising out of the First World War first appeared in treaties of pacific settlement.[6] To assure

[3] Such reservations could be classified as coming at the end of the system of the court's jurisdiction or within the instrument of acceptance. See for examples, Max Sorensen, "The International Court of Justice: Its Role in Contemporary International Relations," *International Organization,* vol. 14 (1967), p. 267; Ruth C. Lawson, "The Problem of Compulsory Jurisdiction of the World Court," *American Journal of International Law,* vol. 46 (1952), p. 237, note 2.

[4] P.C.I.J., Series A/B, No. 74, pp. 10-48 (1938).

[5] I.C.J. Rep. (1952), p. 93.

[6] See "Disputes Arising out of the War of 1914" in League of Nations *Arbitration and Security: Systematic Survey of the Arbitration Conventions and Treaties of Mutual Security Deposited with the League of Nations.*

that the United Nations would not be burdened with the peace settlement as the League of Nations had been, the Charter was separated from the peace treaties and Article 107 reserved to the victors the primary responsibility for the terms of the peace and the occupation, as follows:

> Nothing in the present Charter shall invalidate or preclude action, in relation to any state which during the Second World War has been an enemy of any signatory to the present Charter, taken or authorized as a result of that war by the Government having responsibility for such action.

This provision has been advanced several times in an effort to block United Nations consideration of questions, the most notable instance being the Soviet insistence that the Berlin question was outside the competence of the Security Council.[7] The language of the article gives primary responsibility to the victors much more clearly than it bars United Nations agencies from dealing with the subject when disputes arise after the exercise of that primary responsibility. The application of the clause has supported this interpretation, for the international organs have not declined to consider questions when they were faced with the plea that Article 107 removed the matter from their jurisdiction.[8]

DOMESTIC JURISDICTION RESERVATIONS

Writing in 1925 on the subject of domestic jurisdiction, "a new catchword" which was replacing "the somewhat battered idols of sovereignty, state equality, and the like" as an argument against international obligations, J.L. Brierly complained that little seemed to be known about the term except its extreme sanctity.[9] In the intervening years, this overused guardian of the reserved domain of states has been subject to much stress and change. Initially devised to restrict League of Nations recommendations for pacific settlement of disputes arising

[7] Although the matter was raised by France, the United Kingdom, and the United States as a threat to the peace under Chapter VII of the Charter, the debates indicated reliance on procedures for peaceful settlement rather than the application of coercive measures.

[8] For a survey and analysis of early cases, see United Nations *Repertory of Practice of United Nations Organs* (1955), vol. 5, pp. 385-396.

[9] J. L. Brierly, "Matters of Domestic Jurisdiction," *British Yearbook of International Law,* vol. 6 (1925), p. 8.

out of domestic matters, the concept was broadened in the Charter of the United Nations to cover all activities of that international organization.

The plea of domestic jurisdiction has always been more apt to appear than to be effective, for the sanctity noted by Brierly decreased in direct proportion to the distance between each international entity and the locus of the problem which inspired its invocation. Only a state's own affairs are sacrosanct; the affairs of friends and allies deserve some consideration; and the affairs of rivals are fair game. From its inception, the term "domestic jurisdiction" did not lend itself to any one specific definition. Indeed, the plausibility of several different interpretations is perhaps the most obvious conclusion which can be drawn from a study of the term. Even in the *Tunis-Morocco Nationality Decrees case,*[10] regarded by many as the leading case on the subject of domestic jurisdiction, the Permanent Court of International Justice did not attempt a definition more complete than was necessary for the solution of that particular case. In the organs of the United Nations, where delegates have often spoken about the domestic jurisdiction of states, the usual pattern has been simply to state that the dispute or situation under discussion arises out of a matter which is or is not within the domestic jurisdiction of the state concerned. Although a delegate does, on occasion, attempt to define the term, there is a general tendency to avoid definition. When the dispute between Iran and the United Kingdom over the Iranian government's nationalization of the Anglo-Iranian Oil Company was dropped from the agenda of the Security Council, the delegate of Brazil expressed relief that the Council would not "be confronted with the difficult problem of defining the concept of domestic jurisdiction." [11] A general statement on the meaning of "domestic jurisdiction" or on the content of the domestic jurisdiction of states is, however, possible. In the broadest sense, the domestic jurisdiction of a state comprises those matters concerning which it has a right to act with discretion. In a more technical legal sense, the domestic jurisdiction of a state comprises those matters in which it can act without regulation by international law.

The basic problem in defining domestic jurisdiction is that of determining whether to approach it from an objective or subjective point of view. An objective determination of the scope of domestic jurisdiction involves nothing more than an objective study of the content of inter-

[10] P.C.I.J., Series B, No. 4.

[11] S.C.O.R. 6th Year, 563rd Meeting, p. 40.

national law, for, thus defined, domestic jurisdiction comprises those matters not covered by international law. With equal claim to objectivity, since it relies on international law as a criterion, is the approach which holds that domestic jurisdiction is the sphere in which international law allows each state to be the sole judge.

The subjective approaches to domestic jurisdiction fall into no neat categories. They range from attempts to equate domestic jurisdiction with, or make it a function of, sovereignty and national independence to definitions that cynically attempt to avoid obligations. The greater part of those who approach domestic jurisdiction subjectively at the present time appear to define it as that group of matters which are too insignificant to have international repercussions. This approach, which is related to the doctrine of international concern, recognizes that the international repercussions (the extent of the repercussions may vary) of a matter may remove it from domestic to international jurisdiction. Occasionally, domestic jurisdiction is defined both objectively and subjectively as "questions of sovereignty and all differences the settlement of which is left by international law to the exclusive competence of each state" [12] or as matters which have not become the subject of international obligations or which are not a potential or actual threat to international peace and security.[13]

Since its first appearance in an international organization's constituent act, these possibilities for varying interpretations of domestic jurisdiction have resulted in shifting interpretations of the concept, none of which has seriously limited international jurisdiction and reduced the obligations that flow from membership.

Objective Application of the League Reservation

As it first appeared in Article 15 (8) of the Covenant, the domestic jurisdiction reservation introduced a legal (objective) criterion in the phrase "which by international law is solely within the domestic jurisdiction." Although this would appear to have laid the foundation for exemption of states from international interference in matters not clearly regulated by international law, two other factors contributed materially to an opposite result. First, the clause also authorized League organs to decide the question of competence and the members could not resist

[12] *For. Rel.*, vol. 3 (1928), pp. 949-950.

[13] H. Lauterpacht, *International Law and Human Rights*, (New York: Frederick A. Praeger, 1950), pp. 213-215.

the temptation to intervene. Secondly, the very nature of the reservation almost automatically forecloses the possibility that a state will avoid the "obligation" of having its problem discussed in an international forum. This second point requires amplification.

The reason for the inherent failure of the reservation to accomplish the purpose of its users results from the fact that two different competences are involved—that of the state and that of the international organ. The determination of the first competence is a question of a substantive nature which can be decided only by an examination of the obligations of a state to determine whether it is free to act with discretion. The determination of the second competence (often regarded as a preliminary question) should follow the determination of the first, for the obvious intention of the domestic jurisdiction reservation is to declare the lack of competence of international organs in matters in which states are free to act with discretion.[14] Whether the international organ has been a legal or a political agency, there has resulted a practice of joining the question of competence to the merits of the case. As illustrated in the *Right of Passage Over Indian Territory* case, a plea of domestic jurisdiction both on the preliminary question of competence and on the merits failed although the defendant, on the merits, was later found not to have acted contrary to its obligations.

Once the international organ is seized of the case, such technical findings as the relevance of the law involved impel the international organ further into the case before the plea of domestic jurisdiction can be disposed of. Thus, the reservation opens up a thorough examination of the case before a recommendation can be made. During the period in which the Covenant reservation was applied with emphasis on the legal concept of domestic jurisdiction, it served in no case to bar a final recommendation, for international organs were unwilling to be stopped by it.

Although its location in Article 15 limited its application, strictly speaking, to the League procedures of arbitration, members invoked its limitations in many situations not involving disputes or pacific settlement (such as world economic or social problems). There is evidence

[14] For an elaboration of this and related technical points, see John M. Howell "Delimiting 'Domestic Jurisdiction'," *The Western Political Quarterly*, vol. 10 (1957), pp. 512-526 and John M. Howell and Robert R. Wilson, "The Commonwealth and Domestic Jurisdiction," *American Journal of International Law*, vol. 55 (1961), pp. 29-44.

that it was only in the latter use that the reservation served as a limitation on the scope of the League's powers.[15]

The Subjective Charter Formula

After the Second World War, states accepted more fully than ever the collective security concept that no matter threatening or breaching international peace and security can be reserved from international jurisdiction. Furthermore, when the San Francisco Conference met to establish a United Nations with authority to eradicate the underlying causes of war, the organization was given new and ill-defined powers relating to human rights, non-self-governing territories, and economic and social cooperation. In a move to counter this advance in international jurisdiction, the domestic jurisdiction reservation was transferred from the section on pacific settlement of disputes to Article 2 where it applies to all United Nations activities, and the exception at the end of the reservation was amended for the express purpose of limiting international activity in situations arising from domestic matters to enforcement measures under Chapter VII. This had the immediate effect of confusing the dividing line between international and domestic jurisdictions, for the limitation on international jurisdiction seemed to apply to situations the continuance of which is likely to endanger the maintenance of international peace and security (Chapter VI), to recommendations for peaceful settlement of situations that constitute a threat to the peace (Chapter VII), and to efforts to ameliorate the many problems that might arise in connection with human rights, non-self-governing territories, and economic and social cooperation.

The resultant weakness and ambiguity of substantive law covering the foregoing areas of international involvement were offset by the determination of decision-making majorities to use United Nations machinery in the interest of peace. Employing ambiguity to expand rather than to restrict, they developed a justification for increasing international activity by the development, one a case-by-case basis, of a new meaning of international concern. Often referred to as the "doctrine of international concern," it became a device to substitute emergency powers when substantive law relating to the above-mentioned areas is inadequate.

[15] John M. Howell, "Domestic Jurisdiction," in Robert R. Wilson, *et al, The International Law Standard and Commonwealth Developments* (Durham: Duke University Press, 1966), pp. 141-146.

Beginning with the discussion regarding the relationship of United Nations members with the Franco regime in Spain and continuing through the perennial debates on South African racial policies, the argument that a matter is removed from domestic jurisdiction if its repercussions can be termed a potential threat to the peace was perfected. A potential threat appears to be closer to the situations described in Chapter VI of the Charter than to those in Chapter VII, for it was originally described as a situation within the meaning of Article 34. But is was apparently more serious and immediate than the usual situation in that category, removing the matter from domestic jurisdiction, whereas cases instituted under Article 34 were ordinarily subject to the domestic jurisdiction reservation. One writer has suggested that United Nations organs have overridden challenges to their jurisdiction based on domestic jurisdiction in problems that were the out-growth of large-scale, systematic discriminatory practices of one form or another.[16] Presumably challenges based on domestic jurisdiction in problems that were the outgrowth of incidental discriminatory practices could succeed because the situation would only be one the continuance of which is likely to endanger peace.

It suffices to point out here that the doctrine of international concern immediately made available the procedures of pacific settlement even if a party raised the plea of domestic jurisdiction. After United Nations membership had been extended to the states newly emerged from colonial status, the doctrine was regarded as removing the domestic jurisdiction restriction from any case involving non-self-governing territories and systematic racial discrimination.

At the time of the Congo crisis, the expansion of international obligations assumed a new dimension. When United Nations forces in the Congo assumed responsibility for such activities as maintenance of local law and order, a significant portion of the reserved domain of a national state was under international jurisdiction. The shift from national to international jurisdiction had previously been of a horizontal nature, simply a broadening of topics regarding which an international organ could discuss and recommend to governments. In the Congo situation the shift was vertical, or in depth, for the United Nations bypassed the national government to deal directly with the people and, when the national government finally objected, its objections were generally ignored.

[16] Thomas Buergenthal, "The United Nations and the Development of Rules Relating to Human Rights," *Proceedings of the American Society of International Law*, 1965, p. 132.

Expanding International Control by a Return to International Rules

The Rhodesian crisis illustrates a shift from reliance on international concern as a basis for international jurisdiction back to an examination of the body of international law to determine if it removes a matter from domestic jurisdiction. This development has been hastened by an expanded membership which has reordered the hierarchy of international values and has assumed that repeated General Assembly resolutions on racial and colonial matters have created new international laws.[17] The case also demonstrates an effort to increase the effectiveness of international efforts to resolve the issues in Rhodesia by declaring the matter a threat to international peace, thereby increasing the sanctions available to the international organization.

The alternative possibilities of defeating domestic jurisdiction pleas by reliance on substantive law or by emphasizing international concern for the international repercussions of a situation have been available since the League of Nations went into operation, with the former in the ascendancy until the resolution of the jurisdictional question in the case of *Relations Between Members of the United Nations and Spain.* The Rhodesian case marks the beginning of a trend to return to a substantive-law basis for jurisdiction. While the doctrine of international concern accommodates rapid development of international institutions by decision-making majorities, salutary stability of the law is suggested when this emergency powers justification is supplanted by new consensus on substantive rules. The extension of this consensus to other doubtful areas of jurisdiction remains to be assessed, for this case only demonstrates that the world community no longer regards the establishment of a racist state out of a colonial territory as a question for the exclusive decision-making of the elites in that area.

CONCLUSION

In summary, the major clause which states have developed to protect themselves from international organization has been a poor guarantor, so poor, in fact, that its invocation now appears to be more for the

[17] For one analysis of this method of developing international law see, Samuel A. Bleicher, "The Legal Significance of Re-Citation of General Assembly Resolutions," *American Journal of International Law,* vol. 63 (1969), pp. 444-478.

satisfaction of public opinion in the objecting state than from the hope that it will convince colleagues in international organs. This failure of the clause has remained constant as its interpretations have shifted from a relatively objective application during the League period, through a frankly political and subjective approach during the first two decades of the United Nations, to a beginning of a return to a more legal application in the Rhodesian case. This constancy is due to a major change in international organization membership which has pressed for the acceptance of the argument that international law has developed to regulate many matters which have been traditionally domestic and which has refused to accept the view that sovereignty (especially of the Western World with its "older international law") could be interposed to block the attempt to resolve questions involving racial discrimination and colonialism.

Because domestic jurisdiction reservations are poor devices for avoiding international obligations within the orderly framework of international organizations, it appears that states will either resort to noncompliance and defiance or reduce their memberships in such organizations.

A little progress toward a viable system of resolving these issues within the orderly framework of international organizations could be made by a mutual realization that reservations commonly available are scarcely sufficient to calm the fears of states most willing to enter international organizations. A little more progress could be made by a mutual acceptance of the principle that the international need for better procedures for maintaining peace and security must be balanced with the states' requirement that some questions will not be artificially classified as critical in order to come within international competence. The drafting of a reservation or reservations that will objectively embody that principle is a project that justifies our most careful consideration, and a recent session of the American Society of International Law has touched on this question in a discussion of means of persuading governments to accept procedural solutions.[18] It seems, however, that a proposal made there to draft a "veto" reservation authorizing a party to decline for national security reasons to accept a solution after it has been offered [19] is a step backward instead of forward. This would be nothing more than a legitimization of techniques of avoiding or defying obligations that are

[18] Fourth Session, *Proceedings of the American Society of International Law,* 1964.

[19] Roger Fisher, "The Veto As a Means of Making Third-Party Settlement Acceptable," *Proceedings of the American Society of International Law,* 1964, pp. 123-129.

dealt with in other chapters of this study. What is needed is something similar to the objectively interpreted domestic jurisdiction reservation and the narrowly interpreted prior disputes reservation. If this is too much to ask in the context of current power struggles, we might begin even more modestly by recognizing that many reservations precisely stated and capable of objective application are better than one vague reservation susceptible to subjective interpretation—better for the international community and for the state.

CHAPTER V

ILLUSTRATIONS OF FAILURE OF DOMESTIC JURISDICTION TO PREVENT AN INCREASE IN OBLIGATIONS

INTRODUCTION

Although the plea of domestic jurisdiction has been entered with great frequency in discussions of disputes and situations before international organs, the development of its effectiveness, or ineffectiveness, has been confined to a few leading cases. Beginning with the *Tunis-Morocco Nationality Decrees* case during the League period, these cases will be described in this and the following chapter. They are presented as an elaboration and substantiation of the failure of the plea of domestic jurisdiction as a means of avoiding international obligations which has been described in the preceding chapter. Since the cases in this chapter collectively describe the trend in international organs to expand their jurisdiction horizontally to include additional topics that are subject to the discussion and recommendation functions of international organs, each can be described with some brevity. The subtleties by which the Congo crisis illustrates a vertical expansion, or direct international organ involvement in the affairs of a state, require the more detailed coverage of the following chapter.

THE TUNIS-MOROCCO NATIONALITY DECREES

In 1921, the Bey of the French Protectorate of Tunis and the President of the French Republic each issued a decree affecting the nationality of certain persons born in Tunis. If a person's parents were born in Tunis and were subject to French courts, French nationality was imposed on him. If his parents were born in Tunis, but were not subject to French courts, Tunisian nationality was imposed on him. A considerable number of British subjects, principally of Maltese origin, were resident in Tunisia at this time. Since they and their parents were subject to the jurisdiction of the French courts, in common with other Europeans there, they became French nationals under the new decrees. Similar decrees were issued in Morocco but were not immediately applicable to British subjects.

Military service was an obligation of French nationality and British subjects were called up for service in the French army. Some resisted conscription and were imprisoned. The British government protested to the French government and the question finally came before the Permanent Court of International Justice for an advisory opinion on the jurisdiction of the League Council to hear the case. The French government argued before the Court that the Council was incompetent because the dispute arose from a domestic matter.

The representative of the complaining state, Great Britain, said in his opening statement before the Court that a preliminary question was involved and that he would not attempt to make good his various contentions on the merits of the case.[1] In his argument, the British representative made two points. (1) In the event of a dispute between two states in which a party relies on international treaty rights, the other party cannot make a unilateral finding that no such right exists. The dispute over the *existence of the right* is not within domestic jurisdiction. (2) Once the international organ begins to examine the situation to determine whether there is a right, it must find that the domestic policy complained of *is inconsistent* with the treaty obligations of the state making the policy. After setting forth this distinction, the British representative discarded it and proceeded to argue that the mere fact that the parties to the dispute *allege* international treaty rights removes not only the determination of the nature of the matter in dispute from domestic jurisdiction, but it also removes the matter itself from domestic jurisdiction.

The French representative argued that it would be necessary to discuss the substantive issues involved and he proceeded to examine the treaty provisions relied on by both sides in an effort to show that they did not constitute an international obligation on the part of France.[2]

The Court refused to follow the French argument. In its statement on the finding that was necessary when a domestic jurisdiction plea is entered, the Court provided for a provisional finding when it said:

> ...when once it appears that the legal grounds (*titres*) relied on are such as to justify the provisional conclusion that they are of juridical importance for the dispute sub-

[1] P.C.I.J., Series C, No. 2, p. 23.

[2] *Ibid.*, pp. 215-217.

mitted to the Council, and that the question whether it is competent for one State to take certain measures is subordinated to the formation of an opinion with regard to the validity and construction of these legal grounds (*titres*), the provisions contained in paragraph 8 of Article 15 cease to apply and the matter, ceasing to be one solely within the domestic jurisdiction of the State, enters the domain governed by international law.[3]

The Court has here defined the sphere of a state's domestic jurisdiction in a substantive manner, by saying, in effect, that it is the sphere not regulated by international law or treaty law; but it has proceeded to define the Council's jurisdiction in a manner that does not require a complete finding on the individual state's freedom from obligation. The Council's jurisdiction begins when once the legal grounds relied on justify the *provisional conclusion that they are of juridical importance for the dispute*. This is simply a finding that the legal grounds relied on have *some* relevance to the case. The degree of relevance that was necessary in this particular case was slight. In its examination of the legal grounds relied on by the parties, the Court concluded in each instance that a decision on the opposing contentions necessitated an examination of international law; therefore, the question was no longer solely within domestic jurisdiction. Regarding one of the French arguments, the Court said: "Since, *even assuming the French contention to be correct,* the question whether France possessed such competence... would still depend...on the construction to be placed upon the most-favored-nation clause," this question is not domestic.[4]

Although this and other cases involving domestic jurisdiction during the interwar period did not clarify further the problems of applying domestic jurisdiction reservations (particularly those regarding the degree in which a state must be obligated in order for its discretion to be limited), there was an underlying assumption that the League of Nations organs should determine the substantive content of domestic jurisdiction of the parties to a dispute before declaring their own competence.

The tendency of the League to prefer legal procedures is well known, but a preference for legal procedures did not lead to a rigid definition of "domestic jurisdiction." Reference to specific content of that sphere did point the way to a static definition, but the League seemed to prefer a flexible statement of principle that could be applied by non-political agencies in each case that arose.

[3] *Ibid.*, Ser. B, No. 4, p. 26.

[4] *Ibid.*, pp. 28-32, Italics added.

THE QUESTION OF RELATIONS OF MEMBERS OF THE UNITED NATIONS WITH SPAIN

The shift from an objective (legal) to a subjective (political) interpretation of the domestic jurisdiction reservation, which was initiated by the language of the Charter reservation in Article 2, paragraph 7, received its first elaboration in the discussions regarding the relations of members of the United Nations with Spain.

When the Polish delegate to the Security Council charged in 1946 that the activities of the Franco regime "endangered international peace and security," the Netherlands delegate suggested that the matter was within Spain's domestic jurisdiction. The question was referred to a subcommittee, which reported that the situation in Spain did not constitute a threat to the peace but that it did constitute a situation the continuance of which was likely to endanger the maintenance of international peace and security. In other words, it was a matter in which the domestic jurisdiction reservation would serve to block Security Council action if the matter were domestic. Then the subcommittee proceeded to examine the situation to determine whether it was domestic. Although the subcommittee found no threat to the peace, breach of the peace or act of aggression, it found that the matters brought before the Security Council in relation to Franco Spain were of so serious a nature that the Security Council, in discharging its primary responsibility for the maintenance of international peace and security, should not allow them to pass from its notice simply because it was unable to take the direct enforcement measures proposed in the Polish draft resolution.[5]

The report of the subcommittee went no further than an implication that a matter is removed from domestic jurisdiction when it is involved in a dispute which is a potential threat to the peace, but it is only a short step to an explicit statement to that effect. This step was made by the Australian delegate, Herbert V. Evatt, who was the *Rapporteur* of the subcommittee, when he said:

> When you look at the internal affairs of a country, you start off with the postulate that it is no business of any other nation to concern itself with how the people of that country govern themselves. That is *prima facie*, primarily a matter of domestic concern, but if the facts indicate that that regime, by its nature, by its conduct, by its operations, is likely to interfere with international peace and likely to be a menace

[5] S.C.O.R., 1st year, 1st Series, Special Supplement (Revised Edition), Report of the Sub-Committee on the Spanish Question, pp. 1-2, 8-9.

to its neighbors, then the existence of that regime is no longer a matter of essentially domestic concern. The Charter is built on that basis.[6]

The subcommittee report blurred the already hazy distinction between a dispute the continuance of which is likely to endanger the maintenance of international peace and security (Article 33-38 in Chapter VI, to which the domestic jurisdiction reservation applies) and a threat to the peace (Articles 39-50, in Chapter VII, to which it does not apply if enforcement action is ordered). The Australian delegate built on this confusion and disposed of the applicability of the domestic jurisdiction reservation in the Spanish case even though it was being considered under Chapter VI by saying:

Now, in my opinion, ...it should be pointed out quite clearly that Article 2, paragraph 7 of the Charter does not say that the United Nations should not intervene in any matter which does not fall within Chapter VII. What it does say is that the United Nations shall not intervene in a matter essentially within the domestic jurisdiction of a state... The facts are that there is a situation the continuance of which, in the finding of the Sub-Committee, is likely to endanger the maintenance of international peace and security. That situation has already led to strong expressions of concern and disapproval by various Governments and to the closing of a frontier. There is a record of past participation in the Second World War and of recent action hindering the victorious Allies in removing the vestiges of Nazism. Various Governments, Members of the United Nations, have already broken off diplomatic relations and recognized a rival Government. All this is a matter of vital international concern. The situation, I submit, is the complete antithesis of an essentially domestic situation.[7]

Evatt's construction extended the proviso that the domestic jurisdiction reservation does not cover matters if they constitute a threat to the peace requiring enforcement action to include less explosive situations which are of international concern. In so doing, he made the assumption that these less serious matters, or potential threats to the peace, also cease to be domestic. The argument of the Australian delegate was repeated by other delegates. Once the idea was accepted, it was another short step to a definition of matters within domestic jurisdiction, or domestic questions, as those which were not of international concern. The development of a subjective, or political, concept of domestic jurisdiction was complete.

A potential threat appears to be closer to the situations described in Chapter VI of the Charter than to those in Chapter VII, for it was

[6] S.C.O.R., 1st year, 1st Series, No. 2, pp. 344-345, 353-354.

[7] *Ibid.*, pp. 317-318.

originally described as a situation within the meaning of Article 34. But it is apparently more serious and immediate than the usual situation in that category, removing the matter from domestic jurisdiction, whereas cases instituted under Article 34 are ordinarily subject to the domestic jurisdiction reservation.

It suffices to point out here that the doctrine of international concern immediately made available the procedures of pacific settlement even if a party raised the plea of domestic jurisdiction. Applied in conjunction with such Charter provisions as those on human rights, discrimination, non-self-governing territories, or self-determination, the doctrine of international concern can be employed by decision-making majorities to justify jurisdiction on any matter which they decide has international importance.

THE SOUTH AFRICAN CASES

The initial statement on international concern in the *Spanish* case has been thoroughly elaborated in the perennial discussions of racial discrimination in the Union of South Africa.

India brought the first racial discrimination case to the first session of the General Assembly under the heading of "Treatment of Indians in the Union of South Africa." A few years later India and other Asiatic countries brought an additional charge concerning the South African policy of *apartheid*. In the seventeenth session of the Assembly, the two were jointed and debated together.

South Africa's defense has followed rather closely the legal definition of domestic jurisdiction developed during the League of Nations period. Starting from the premise that a binding legal obligation removes a matter from domestic jurisdiction, the South Africans urged the absence of such obligations. Regarding the bilateral agreements relied on by India, South Africa denied that they were true international agreements; regarding the Charter provisions on human rights, South Africa said they were too vague to be binding.

In its arguments, India has employed and amplified the concept of international concern. India pointed out that reactions in India to the South African policy had been "so serious" that India had to terminate trade arrangements and recall its high commissioner. The situation was "likely to impair friendly relations." Furthermore, the South African treatment violated fundamental principles of the Charter, and India had "moral and political obligations" toward the South Africans of Indian ancestry. Although India relied on the Capetown Agreement between India and South Africa (negotiated in 1927 and renewed in 1932 to protect Indians in South Africa), the Indian appeal said the question was "a political and not a legal one." Its "potential consequences" made it a world problem, and the United Nations must exercice its "moral sanction" to solve it.[8]

When the South African delegate made reference to inapplicability of the Charter obligations on human rights, the Indians argued that such obligations did not have to be spelled out in detail and that South Africa was obligated to undertake compliance by virtue of being a party to the resolution protesting against racial persecution and discrimination then recently adopted by the General Assembly.[9]

In the third session of the General Assembly, the Indian delegate clearly added the repercussions argument to the other bases for international jurisdiction by referring to the "very tense situation" created by the African policy and the "gravest consequences" of it outside Africa. If allowed to continue, he said, it "would become a potential threat to the peace." [10]

Thirteen Asiatic countries introduced the question of "Race Conflict in South Africa Resulting from the Policy of Apartheid" by saying that it was creating a dangerous and explosive situation, which constituted both a threat to international peace and a flagrant violation of the basic principles of human rights and fundamental freedoms.[11] India made passing reference to obligations, but the emphasis clearly was on repercussions. India referred to "a dangerous tension...imperilling the entire continent of Africa" and "widespread indignation." In a rare attempt to define a potential threat to the peace, the Indian delegate said that:

> The concept of a threat to peace was not confined to the case of a threat to the territorial integrity and political independence of a State. A threat to peace might assume various forms. A situation where there might be only a potential threat to peace was nonetheless likely to endanger the maintenance of international peace. Flagrant breaches of human rights by the government of a State would have serious repercussions outside that State and could affect international peace.[12]

[8] G.A.O.R., 1st Series, pt 2, Joint Committee of the 1st and 6th Committees (1946), pp. 3, 52-53.

[9] *Ibid.*, pp. 10-12.

[10] *Ibid.*, 3rd Sess., pt. 2, vol. 1 (1949), p. 438.

[11] *Ibid.*, 7th Sess., vol. II, Annexes II, Agenda Item No. 66 (1952-53), p. 2.

[12] *Ibid.*, vol. V, Ad Hoc Political Committee (1952-53), pp. 67-68, 96.

In the thirteenth session of the Assembly, Ghana introduced the question by saying that since racialism was a threat to the very foundations of international peace and security, no member of the United Nations should be allowed to prevent discussion on the question on the pretext that it was domestic. He termed the South African policy an "affront to the conscience of the civilized world" that had "repercussions on race relations everywhere." He said that he wondered if anyone could continue to doubt that the question of race conflict had become "such a threat to the peace as to constitute a matter of international concern." [13] In the fifteenth session of the General Assembly, the Nigerian delegate said that the patience of his government was exhausted and that racial discrimination could never be regarded as being within domestic jurisdiction.[14]

Although the debates have continued they have added nothing to the meaning of domestic jurisdiction. It was not until the Rhodesian case that the removal of racial discrimination from domestic jurisdiction was assumed to have been accomplished by the development of new international law on that subject. This change was stated in an atmosphere more clearly distinguishable from the earlier proposition that an "emergency" jurisdiction is created by the grave international repercussions of a situation. This shift from "emergency" jurisdiction to jurisdiction based on new law has not been sudden. The arguments of opposing states have advanced both points in all cases. The distinction is one of emphasis. In the earlier cases, the majority spoke of the gravity and urgency of the situation and the overriding need for the organization to maintain peace. In the Rhodesian case, the initial emphasis was on the international legal obligations that states now have. Calls for maintenance of world peace were usually coupled with suggestions that stronger enforcement measures were required.

THE RHODESIAN CASE

Challenges to international jurisdiction in the Rhodesian case were brushed aside by decision-making majorities intent on negotiating the passage of resolutions with sufficient force to bring about the collapse

[13] *Ibid.*, 13th Sess., Special Political Committee (1958), p. 7.
[14] *Ibid.*, 15th Sess., Special Political Committee, p. 41.

of the "illegal racist minority regime" of Prime Minister Ian Smith. From the time of the adoption of the Declaration on the Granting of Independence to Colonial Countries and Peoples until the declaration of independence by the Smith regime on November 11, 1965, the United Nations had acted on the assumption that the status of non-self-governing territories was an international question. Addition of the factors of racial discrimination and undemocratic political systems to the anti-colonial base provided an atmosphere in which legalistic arguments against international jurisdiction carried little weight. The serious debate passed over the question of international competence and concentrated on the justification of sanctions capable of bringing about a change of government in Salisbury. Application of the doctrine of international concern was barely discernible in justifications of international competence over the Rhodesian issue before November 11; after that date the considerable attention given to international repercussions to be expected as a result of the Smith regime was not aimed at the jurisdictional question. The situation was finally declared a threat to international peace, not to circumvent the restrictions of Article 2 (7) but to make available the sanctions of Chapter VII of the Charter.

The illustration of these statements requires a survey of developments before and after November 11 that relate to the jurisdictional questions and the application of sanctions.

The dispute over the capacity of Chapter XI of the Charter (Declaration Regarding Non-Self-Governing Territories) to add to international jurisdiction and thereby remove colonial questions from domestic jurisdiction culminated in the 1960 Declaration on Granting Independence to Colonial Countries and Peoples. Preambular paragraphs of the Declaration mentioned Charter provisions on human rights and equal rights as well as self-determination of peoples and noted that increasing conflicts resulting from denial of such rights constitute a serious threat to world peace.[15] So much emphasis has been placed on the international repercussions approach (doctrine of international concern) in justifying international jurisdiction since the Spanish case began in 1946 that the possibility that new international rules remove a matter from domestic jurisdiction is often overlooked. Yet this possibility was clearly indicated in the Covenant reference to questions which by international law are domestic and by the Court's much-quoted advisory opinion on the *Tunis-Morocco Nationality Decrees* case.

[15] A/Res. 1514 (XI), 14 December 1960.

Reference to a threat to peace in the preamble of the Declaration on Granting Independence to Colonial Countries and Peoples is a hold-over from the days when the decision-making majorities questioned the force of Charter provisions on human rights and non-self-governing territories and developed the doctrine of international concern to increase their enabling power. But the membership of the United Nations in 1960 was unwilling to doubt international jurisdiction on these subjects. Operative paragraphs of the Declaration, seeking to apply Charter statements relative to ending colonial control over non-self-governing territories, indicate further that the decision-making majority sought to apply Charter provisions in this area without reference to international peace.

In the following year, the General Assembly moved to apply the Declaration by questioning the self-governing status of Rhodesia. After a year of intermittent debate in the General Assembly and its Special Committee of Seventeen to consider whether Rhodesia was self-governing, the Assembly passed a resolution which did not rely on a threat to international peace. The Special Committee noted that the situation was grave and called for action to prevent a drift toward upheaval and conflict, but the Assembly resolution deplored the denial of equal political rights and liberties of a vast majority, affirmed that the territory was non-self-governing, and requested the United Kingdom to convene a constitutional conference with full participation of all political parties to formulate a new constitution which would insure rights of the majority of the people on the basis of one man one vote.[16]

United Kingdom protests that Rhodesia's status as a self-governing territory barred both the government in London and the United Nations from intervening to change local legislation and barred all except the administering power from the decision on complete independence fell on unsympathetic ears. As negotiation between London and Salisbury broke down and the Smith government moved toward a unilateral declaration of independence, the Council, Assembly, and the Assembly's Special Committee repeatedly exercised competence over the matter. In a resolution passed in the month preceding the Rhodesian declaration of independence, the General Assembly expressed concern over the perpetuation of a minority rule which would be incompatible with the principle of equal rights and self-determination of peoples proclaimed in the Charter and the Declaration of 1960 and called upon the United Kingdom to take all possible measures to prevent a unilateral declaration of independence

[16] A/Res. 1747 (XVI), 28 June 1962.

and, in the event of such a declaration to take all steps necessary to put an immediate end to rebellion.[17] Less than one month later, the Assembly referred to the increasing cooperation between Rhodesia, South Africa, and Portugal as a "threat to freedom, peace and security in Africa" and called upon the United Kingdom to "employ all necessary measures, including military force" to bring about the repeal of specified repressive measures of the Smith regime, suspend the 1961 Constitution, and institute new constitutional arrangements on the basis of universal adult suffrage.[18] This finding of a threat to peace in Africa was not needed to validate the goals of this resolution, but it added a sense of urgency.

Through the device of recalling previous resolutions, the international agencies maintained the basis of the original resolution on Rhodesia. References to international repercussions of varying degrees of seriousness in the period before November 11 may have been motivated by the simple conclusion that the situation was dangerous or by a desire to increase the pressure on the United Kingdom to block the plans of the Smith regime to declare independence. Since the United Kingdom could act in Rhodesia without a finding of a threat to international peace and the United Nations had already announced and exercised its competence to call upon the United Kingdom to move its colony toward independence under Charter provisions on non-self-governing territories the latter motivation is more plausible.

When the issue shifted from blocking Rhodesian plans for a declaration of independence to bringing pressure to defeat a form of government that the majority of United Nations members found obnoxious, the motivation was less elusive. The General Assembly and Security Council immediately passed brief resolutions condemning the "unilateral declaration of independence made by a racist minority in Southern Rhodesia."[19] In a later resolution to institute severance of diplomatic and economic relations between members and Rhodesia, and particularly to embargo shipments of oil and petroleum products to the latter, the Council determined that the situation resulting from the declaration of independence was "extremely grave and that its continuance in time constitutes a threat to international peace and security."[20] This language approxim-

[17] A/Res. 2012 (XX), 12 October 1965.
[18] A/Res. 2022 (XX), 5 November 1965.
[19] A/Res. 2024 (XX), 11 November 1965; S/Res. 216, 12 November 1965.
[20] S/Res. 217, 20 November 1965.

ates more closely the Chapter VI reference to disputes the continuance of which is likely to endanger the maintenance of international peace and security than the Chapter VII classification of threats to the peace. Apparently the decision-makers did not feel obliged to declare a threat to peace to circumvent domestic jurisdiction limitations. Neither did they wish at that time to invoke Chapter VII in order to authorize the use of force.

In the following Spring, the Council was in a mood to employ more effective measures to stop the shipments of oil to a rebel government that had not collapsed as soon as expected. A resolution passed at the request of the United Kingdom determined that the situation resulting from supplies of oil which would enable the "illegal regime" to "remain longer in being" would "constitute a threat to peace." In addition to calling upon Portugal and all other states to divert oil destined for Rhodesia, the Council called upon the United Kingdom to use force if necessary and empowered that government to arrest the tanker which was carrying a load of oil to be discharged at Beira, Mozambique, and pumped through the pipeline to Rhodesia.[21]

Members of the Council concerned themselves with whether that body would lend its prestige to the limited course proposed by the British or follow the demands of African delegations for a general use of force to topple the Smith government. The finding of a threat to peace was clearly to give force to the oil embargo rather than to establish that the question was not a domestic one.

In December 1966, the Council extended its call for selective mandatory sanctions on critical commodities. At the suggestion of the United Kingdom it specified that it was acting under Articles 39 and 41 of Chapter VII, which limits the Council to measures not involving the use of armed force.[22] Noting that economic sanctions had failed to "bring down the racist regime," the General Assembly in November of 1967 condemned the United Kingdom for failing to take more effective measures and called for the employment of all measures, including the use of force, to put and end to the Smith regime.[23] After protracted consideration of the ineffectiveness of past measures, the Council, in May of 1968, voted comprehensive mandatory economic sanctions.[24]

[21] S/Res. 221, 9 April 1966.
[22] S/Res. 232, 16 December 1966.
[23] A/Res. 2262 (XXII), 3 November 1967.
[24] S/Res. 253, 29 May 1968.

The success of the measures remains to be seen; but regardless of the outcome, the application of comprehensive mandatory sanctions in a situation once regarded as domestic indicates a significant effort toward establishing effective control over topics that have moved from domestic to international jurisdiction. Obviously, sanctions could also be employed in a matter which has ceased to be protected by the domestic jurisdiction reservation by virtue of becoming a threat or a potential threat to the peace. In this case, however, the assessment of the international gravity of the situation was scarcely related to the question of jurisdiction and was clearly for the purpose of justifying more coercive measures to achieve the end of changing the form of government in a country.

It is, of course, still possible to claim that the United Nations organs lacked competence to pass this variety of resolutions regarding Rhodesia. If the provisions of the Charter regarding non-self-governing territories are interpreted strictly and if the domestic jurisdiction reservation is applied as a bar to United Nations resolutions on any subject not clearly and expressly regulated by international legal rules, the Rhodesian resolutions are not in accordance with the Charter and therefore need not be obeyed (Article 25). Rhodesia obviously takes this position. But on the other hand, the resolutions themselves demonstrate that the decision-making majorities in the United Nations do assume that these resolutions are pursuant to the Charter in its current meaning. They passed them in the face of the objection that the matter was domestic and outside United Nations competence. The argument that the resolutions deal with domestic matters depends on a static interpretation of the Charter which has received scant support and can be maintained only in a legal vacuum apart from the realities and dynamics of international politics.

If there was ever any doubt that the Rhodesian government, as a nonmember, was not obligated to recognize the resolutions, that doubt was legally resolved when the Security Council declared the matter a threat to international peace and authorized the use of force to put an end to the Smith regime. This action undoubtedly brings Article 2 (6) of the Charter into play.

The gap between United Nations aspirations to impose order on the world and its capacity to do so is vast. But lack of effectiveness does not erase legal competence of international organs. By the nature of international organizations, their reach exceeds their grasp. The Rhodesian case, of course, demonstrates that the United Nations lacks the collective will to go past a call for an end to the Smith regime to coercive measures to topple it. But the case also represents a heightened effort to increase the effectiveness of resolutions that deal with matters which were once domestic by raising the issue of international peace. In this sense it is an attempt, not yet successful, to resolve the conflicts of international organizations and states in favor of the international organization.

CHAPTER VI

DIRECT INTERVENTION INTO DOMESTIC AFFAIRS BY THE UNITED NATIONS

INTRODUCTION

When United Nations forces in the Congo assumed responsibility for such activities as maintenance of local law and order, a significant portion of the reserved domain of a national state was under international jurisdiction. The shift from national to international jurisdiction had previously been of a horizontal nature, simply an addition to the topics an international organ could discuss for the purpose of recommending to governments procedures for settlement of disputes or solutions to problems. In the Congo situation the shift was vertical, or in depth, for the United Nations bypassed the national government to deal directly with the people.

Without referring to distinctions between horizontal and vertical changes in jurisdiction, the delegates who wrote the Charter at San Francisco expressed concern for vertical encroachments on domestic jurisdiction. Speaking for the four sponsoring governments, John Foster Dulles emphasized the principle that the Organization would deal with governments and not penetrate directly into the domestic life and economy of the member states.[1] Although expansion in international jurisdiction had been horizontal until the Congo crisis, the speed of that expansion had fostered an atmosphere for rather casual and rapid determination of the jurisdictional question. When the situation rapidly worsened in the Congo, the precedent was already established for further encroachments on domestic jurisdiction without a prolonged constitutional argument.

United Nations forces became increasingly involved in domestic affairs on the basis of decisions by the Secretary-General and the Security

[1] U.N.C.I.O., Doc. 1019 I/1/42, June 16, 1945, p. 1.

Council that had to be made before agreement could be reached on whether the situation was serious enough to override the principle of non-intervention in domestic jurisdiction. The legal problem was compounded by the difficulty of separating the domestic effects of a civil war (and the attendant breakdown of law and order) from the threat to international peace that the war might also pose. The domestic jurisdiction concept would not bar United Nations actions to restore or maintain international peace, but it would (as Security Council resolutions recognized) bar actions to resolve local problems. Furthermore, many delegates appeared to be as strongly motivated to act for the humanitarian purpose of protecting individuals as for maintenance of peace and security.

A description of this vertical shift in the Congo crisis can be limited to (1) the authorization of and limitation on United Nations action in the Security Council and General Assembly resolutions, (2) the use of international forces in the civil strife between Katanga province and the Central Government, (3) the United Nations dilemma in the contention between President Joseph Kasavubu and Premier Patrice Lumumba for recognition as leader of the established Central Government, and (4) the involvement of international agencies in urging actions upon recognized national leaders or in blocking actions those leaders planned to take.

AUTHORIZATION AND LIMITATIONS OF RESOLUTIONS

The first resolutions on the Congo were passed in July, 1960, after Central Government (Leopoldville) leaders (Kasavubu and Lumumba) accused Belgium of encouraging the secession of Katanga and asked United Nations aid to protect the territory of the Congo against external aggression (not to restore internal law and order). In his initial statement to the Security Council, the Secretary-General said that the difficulties in the Congo were "connected with the maintenance of order in the country and the protection of life" and that the presence of Belgian troops was "a source of internal, and potentially international, tension." The Italian delegate spoke of intervention to protect human rights.[2] Thus, several bases of international action were available: request of the government concerned, the potential international tension caused by unrequested Belgian troops, maintenance of order (local) and the human-

[2] S.C.O.R., 873rd meeting, pp. 3-4, 23.

itarian purpose of rescuing those caught between the fighting forces. The Security Council resolution authorizing the Secretary-General to send military assistance (*Operation des Nations Unies au Congo,* or ONUC) and calling for Belgian withdrawal referred to the report of the Secretary-General on a request for United Nations action and the request for assistance addressed to the Secretary-General by the Prime Minister of the Republic of the Congo.[3]

The need to clarify the basis of action must have been immediately apparent, for the Secretary-General elaborated the point on July 18. In his report to the Security Council, he said that it was *implied* in his presentation prior to the passage of the first resolution by that body that the breakdown of the instruments of Congolese government created a situation the consequences of which constituted a threat to the peace justifying United Nations intervention "on the basis of the explicit request of the Government of the Republic of the Congo." Then he added:

> Thus the two main elements, from the legal point of view were on the one side this request and, on the other hand, the implied finding that the circumstances to which I referred were such as to justify United Nations action under the Charter.[4]

Even at the time he suggested a second basis, the Secretary-General said that the United Nations force was a "temporary security force, present in the Republic of the Congo with the consent of the Government." He conceded that the viewpoint of the host Government was "one of the most serious factors which would guide recruitment of personnel" although final decision would rest with the international organ.[5] Neither the Secretary-General's statement nor the first resolution of the Council distinguishes the domestic effects of the civil war from the threat to international peace that the war might also impose. Furthermore the finding of a threat to international peace was very tentative. United Nations action was not based on a threat to the peace alone but on a threat which justified United Nations action on the basis of a request of the local government.

This vagueness recurred in the second resolution of the Council, for again the Council did not directly declare that a threat existed; it "considered" that "the complete restoration of law and order in the Republic

[3] U. N. Doc. S/4387.
[4] S.C.O.R., 887th meeting, p. 2.
[5] *Ibid.,* pp. 2-5.

of the Congo would effectively contribute to the maintenance of international peace and security." [6] Yet by this time ONUC was deeply involved in the domestic scene.

When major power differences forced a transfer of direction from the Security Council to the General Assembly, less reliance was placed on the invitation of the Congolese government. On September 20, an Assembly resolution reaffirming previous Council resolutions and authorizing the Secretary-General "to assist the Central Government of the Congo in the restoration and maintenance of law and order throughout the territory of the Republic" made no reference to an invitation from the Central Government. The resolution took note of the unsatisfactory economic and political conditions in the Congo and spoke of preserving the unity and independence of the Republic, protecting and advancing the welfare of its people, and safeguarding international peace as reasons for United Nations action.[7]

The Assembly resolution seems better designed to include each nation's reason for favoring United Nations action than to clarify the jurisdictional question. In the light of ONUC activities to that time, it appears, however, that United Nations organs regarded themselves competent to maintain local law and order for reasons which included the threat to international peace. At the same time, official United Nations statements to clarify the legal question recognized that a distinction had to be made between involvement in local affairs that was essential to the maintenance of international peace and security and involvement that had the primary result of influencing a decision on a local dispute. From the beginning the Secretary-General stated that ONUC would not take sides in local disputes. The third resolution of the Security Council reaffirmed that position.[8] But events made this technical distinction untenable. The United Nations involvement in the settlement of local conflicts while protesting non-intervention in domestic affairs broadened the gulf between legal arguments and events. If the United Nations is to be regarded as having honored Article 2 (7) of the Charter in the Congo case, it follows that it was not observing the traditional interpretation of that reservation. Although the extent to which international agencies can intervene in domestic affairs to maintain international peace has never been clearly defined, and some involvement in local affairs may be justified as essential

[6] U. N. Doc. S/4405.
[7] U. N. Doc. A/1474 (ES-IV).
[8] U. N. Doc. S/4389, p. 5; U. N. Doc. S/4426.

to the maintenance of international peace, the ONUC action was not a borderline case.

The discrepancy between the legal basis for action and the action that the situation demanded was squarely faced by the delegate of Pakistan before the Security Council. After recognizing the possibility of "endless analysis by the experts of the Charter" in a situation in which world opinion nevertheless expected the United Nations to regulate the situation to the point that it would preserve international peace, he added:

> It is significant that there is before the Council not a single proposal today from any side which does not, in one way or another, involve some kind of interference in matters which would normally be within the essential jurisdiction of the Republic of the Congo. Indeed it would be an exaggeration to say that, despite all controversies between different members of the Council and between various interested Members of the United Nations, a consensus has already emerged that the situation in the Congo is incapable of correction through means which are conventionally within the four corners of the Charter.
> Whether it is the Soviet proposal, or the proposal of Ghana, or even the proposals which are opposed by them, the fact is established that no party visualizes any action in regard to the Congo which would leave its normal domestic jurisdiction intact. Since the fact is so established, we fail to see why, in our thoughts and pronouncements, it must still be evaded and a spurious respect still be shown to the letter of the Charter as it is understood at normal times. If it is not evaded, the United Nations, through the organ of the Security Council must bear open witness to the fact that in an evolving world situation, the United Nations Charter is undergoing historic evolution and that in the matter of the Congo it is called upon to take action of a kind not in accordance with conventional notions of scope and limits.[9]

In the description of the content of domestic jurisdiction, it is not the discrepancy between word and deed but an assessment of the final result that is important. From the vantage point of time, it appears that United Nations majorities, acting under pressure and justifying their actions later, decided that domestic jurisdiction should not prevent their attempt to restore order to the Congo and they acted on that decision. This is only another way of saying that the matter could not be protected by a plea that it was domestic.

[9] U. N. Doc. S/4426.

USE OF INTERNATIONAL FORCES IN THE CIVIL STRIFE

United Nations forces were involved in the civil strife between Katanga province and the Central Government from the outset. Provincial Premier Moise Tshombe requested Belgian troop support and declared that an independent Katanga would retain economic ties with Belgium. By August, the Leopoldville government, dominated by Lumumba, was at odds with the United Nations forces because they would not assist in suppressing the rebellion and Tshombe had notified the Secretary-General that Katanga would resist the entry of United Nations troops into that province. If the international agency sided with either, the other was certain to charge intervention in domestic affairs. Yet, ONUC could not remain aloof or neutral and remain in the Congo.

Tshombe's announcement that Katanga would resist entry of United Nations forces posed a dilemma. Although the Secretary-General regarded the initial Security Council authorization to provide military assistance as applying to the whole of the territory of the Republic, he felt that to override Tshombe's opposition would require military initiative which the United Nations force was not originally given. This prompted a Security Council declaration that the entry of the United Nations Force into the province of Katanga was necessary, but at the same time the Council reaffirmed "that the United Nations Force in the Congo will not be a party to or in any way intervene in or be used to influence the outcome of any internal conflict, constitutional or otherwhise." [10] After negotiations between the Secretary-General and Tshombe, the latter agreed to the entry of forces on the conditions that they not interfere with operations of Katanga police and that arms in the hands of the Katanga army remain under the control of Katanga authorities. This arrangement between Tshombe and the Secretary-General brought bitter attacks from Lumumba without finally ending the secession. In February, 1961, the Council extended the mandate to prevent civil war by authorizing "the use of force, if necessary, as a last resort." [11] With the resolution of the issue over control of the Central government after the death of Lumumba and the appointment of Cyrille Adoula as Prime Minister in August, 1961, the reluctance to use international forces against Katanga gave way to a willingness to act against the rebellious forces. A Security

[10] S.C.O.R., 941st meeting, pp. 61-70.

[11] U. N. Doc. S/4741.

Council resolution in the following November authorized the use of force, if necessary, without requiring that it be a last resort.[12]

As the international agency shifted from a reluctance to a willingness to use force against Katanga it inevitably roused charges of intervention by both sides. The supporters of Tshombe could argue that ONUC prevented the success of the secession in Katanga. The mere statement that the international forces had a role in Katanga or the call for Belgian troop withdrawals related to the solution of the constitutional question. The subsequent authorization and use of force when necessary placed the international organization clearly on the side of the Central government. But on the other hand, the initial entry of international forces into Katanga was based on an agreement with Tshombe and an interpretation of United Nations goals which blocked the Central government from accompanying the international forces or using force to establish its control over the recalcitrant province. In effect, the United Nations position of non-intervention at this stage of the conflict undermined the Central government and questioned its legitimacy.

Although there was much protestation that ONUC would not be a party to or in any way intervene in or be used to influence the outcome of any internal conflict, constitutional or otherwise, the real issue among the protagonists in the Congo and in the United Nations debates was over which side it would favor most. Consideration of the changing content of domestic jurisdiction does not require a value judgment on which side deserved United Nations support. It is sufficient to show that the United Nations, at one time or another, intervened to support both the secessionists and the Central government and to point out that this was no mere horizontal expansion of international jurisdiction.

THE CHOICE BETWEEN KASAVUBU AND LUMUMBA

The activities of the United Nations were further complicated in early September, 1960, when Kasavubu and Lumumba contented for recognition as leader of the Central government. As Lumumba and the Secretary-General clashed over the role of ONUC in Katanga, Lumumba threatened to seek assistance directly from the Soviet Union. Kasavubu's opposition to this course and his continued reliance on the United Nations introduced cold war rivalries directly into the battle for leadership of the Central government.

[12] U. N. Doc. S/5002.

On September 5, Kasavubu dismissed Lumumba as Prime Minister. Lumumba immediately attacked the validity of the President's action and proclaimed that Kasavubu was no longer chief of state. This internal dispute was complicated by the ambiguity of the *Loi fondamentale* regarding the power of these two officers.

The international organization again had to support one or the other if its forces were to remain in the country. The existence of a threat to international peace was clearly recognized by this time, indicating the need as well as the legal justification for international forces in the Congo. But this rationale for international force does not resolve the issue of how far the international agency could become involved in such an internal question as the choice between contending governments. The international organization faced a dilemma. It had to choose between Kasavubu and Lumumba in order to maintain its effectiveness in preserving international peace; to choose between them was intervention in a most important domestic issue.

Demonstrating support for Lumumba, the Soviet Union charged the Secretary-General with favoring Kasavubu and the NATO powers and introduced a resolution which called upon the Secretary-General and ONUC to cease interference in Congolese internal affairs. The resolution was defeated.[13] The Secretary-General, with the apparent support of the majority of the United Nations members, gave qualified support to Kasavubu; he dealt with him as chief of state without recognizing the administrative officials whom he appointed.

It was in the General Assembly debate and decision on the question of seating of representatives of the Republic of the Congo that international involvement in the constitutional question was best demonstrated. Rival factions were aware that international endorsement would strengthen the winner in the constitutional conflict and they waged a bitter fight in the Assembly. When that body seated the Kasavubu delegation on November 22 it took part in the internal conflict.

INVOLVEMENT IN NATIONAL POLICY

After the recognition of the Kasavubu government, the international organization continued to intervene in domestic affairs as it urged actions upon the national leaders or attempted to block their plans.

[13] S.C.O.R., 903rd meeting, p. 17.

Much, but by no means all, of this activity related to the escape of Lumumba from his ONUC guard, his capture by the national army, and his transfer to Katanga where he was killed in mid-February, 1961. Lumumba's escape in late November was followed by an attempt by his supporters to establish a rival central government in Stanleyville. By the end of the year this group, led by Antoine Gizenga, was expanding its control. Kasavubu wanted ONUC assistance in maintaining order and bringing the rebels under control, but he was soon charging that domestic jurisdiction was violated. In February, 1961, the Security Council reacted to the increased threat of widespread civil war caused by the murder of Lumumba by calling for an investigation to ascertain the circumstances of his death to the end that the crime might be punished. It also called for the convening of the Congolese parliament to form a government based on genuine conciliation and for the reorganization of the army. This action by the Council was an impeachment of Central government officials which brought tension to a head and ended any pretense that ONUC was welcomed by local authorities. In March, the Congo objected to the use of Indian troops and said that, since the government of the Congo opposed the Council resolution of February, it should not be implemented until the International Court of Justice ruled that it was valid. In April, while the General Assembly was passing a resolution primarily calling again for Belgian withdrawal, the Congolese proposed the addition at one point of the phrase "with due respect for Congolese sovereignty." The amendment failed, but the resolution passed 61 to 5, with 33 abstentions.[14] The majority either disregarded the domestic jurisdiction reservation or it did not recognize the right of the Central government to exclusive control of Congolese affairs.

APPRAISAL

These events show that the United Nations gave itself an impossible mandate: it could not maintain law and order in the Congo without getting involved in the domestic jurisdiction of the Congo. Whether it acted or refrained from acting, one of the parties in the local dispute would assume that it had favored the other. It was not simply a matter of supervising a truce between orderly opponents; it was a matter of maintaining some law and order while working for a truce. The United

[14] G.A.O.R., 15th Sess., 2nd pt., 985th meeting.

Nations tried to bring about a reorganization of the Congolese army to get it out of politics; it barred local government officials from the use of the nation's radio and airport facilities; in communications, health, finance and other fields, United Nations technical personnel took over to prevent a breakdown of operations. This was intervention in traditionally domestic affairs. The political agencies of the United Nations had little difficulty in recognizing that human rights and international peace were endangered, but they did not find ready precedents for intervening to the extent of running the government if there was such a danger.

It can only be concluded, that in this specific case, due to the exceptionally tense international situation and the weakness of a national government, domestic jurisdiction was diminished to allow the international organization to penetrate directly into the domestic life and economy of a state.

CHAPTER VII

STATE ACTIONS WHEN RELIANCE ON RESERVATIONS FAILS

INTRODUCTION

The three preceding chapters have described the ineffectiveness of reservations as a means of orderly avoidance of obligations voted by international organizations. Decision-making majorities in international organs have never inclined toward protection of state discretion and, as those majorities have increasingly included states with non-white populations fresh from colonialism, they have been even less impressed by suggestions that state sovereignty carries with it a freedom to impose official racial discrimination or deny statehood to colonial areas. This inclination has developed into a tendency to regard many hortatory statements in the Charter as legally binding.

Since this expansion of jurisdiction, with its concomitant possibility of imposing legal or moral obligations, has usually been nothing more forceful than an international organization's activities, lacking the true legislative, executive and judicial powers of government, there would seem to be no great cause for alarm. Nevertheless, states have clearly demonstrated an intention to avoid even this mild sanction when it threatens. They immediately raise arguments against the prospective obligation. As has been noted earlier, of the many possible arguments (the matter at issue is being settled elsewhere, its continuance is not likely to endanger the maintenance of international peace and security, etc.), they have often relied on the domestic jurisdiction reservation, thus making it one of the most-invoked provisions of the Charter.

The vertical expansion of international jurisdiction in the Congo crisis is of a different order, approaching (but not equalling) the effectiveness of an expansion of central government powers in a federal system. In the course of time, a series of Congo-type operations could nullify the domestic jurisdiction concept as a bar to such vertical expansion. Although general sentiment runs against another Congo-type operation, the immediate reaction to its complications cannot be taken as firm evidence that a similar problem will never recur or that world opinion will then oppose another try at solving it. Growing political instability may create the problem and the sentiment to deal with it on the international level.

The Rhodesian case represents an effort to increase the effectiveness of resolutions that deal with matters which have ceased to be domestic by raising the issue of international peace. In this particular case the decision-making majority appeared to conclude that the matter had been removed from domestic jurisdiction for some time and then declared it a threat to peace to increase pressure for settlement. In a future case, the matter could be removed from domestic jurisdiction by virtue of the finding that it is of international concern and, by the same finding, more effective measures could be employed to enforce international decisions regarding it.

The Congo and Rhodesian crises, then, may mark a turning point regarding the reserved domain of states. The period of expansion of international powers to discuss and make resolutions supported by moral force may give way to increases in international control that resemble the transfer of powers from state to national government in a federal system and that amount to more than a transfer from domestic jurisdiction to the jurisdiction of an international organ.

Even before the possibilities of the type of obligations which might be imposed by the precedents of these two cases were evident, states had begun to go outside the orderly processes or international organization to develop patterns for circumventing international obligations. Three such actions will be examined in this chapter: (1) development of reservations which attempt to grant the authority to determine their applicability to the reserving state, (2) simple noncompliance by ignoring or disallowing the obligation,[1] and (3) "walkouts" to express displeasure and to pressure the majority into rescinding the obligation as a means of bringing the recalcitrant state back to active participation.

THE CONNALLY-TYPE DOMESTIC JURISDICTION RESERVATION

Article 36 (6) of the Statute of the International Court of Justice provides that in a dispute as to whether the court has jurisdiction, the

[1] This does not include noncompliance in cases not involving a prior attempt to employ a reservation as an orderly means of avoidance. Such other acts of noncompliance are described in other chapters.

matter shall be settled by the decision of the Court. This follows the wording of the Statute of the predecessor (Permanent Court of International Justice) and the philosophy of the League of Nations reservation of domestic jurisdiction.[2] Domestic jurisdiction reservations to the Optional Clause jurisdiction of the Permanent Court are generally assumed to have implied the Court's power of decision on this point, but after the Second World War, the United States, apparently wary of this possibility, devised a reservation to avoid this threat.

Pursuant to Senate Resolution 196, giving the advice and consent of the Senate to the acceptance of the Optional Clause,[3] the United States declaration provided that the acceptance would not apply to "disputes with regard to matters which are essentially within the domestic jurisdiction of the United States as determined by the United States." [4] A few subsequent reservations correspond to that of the United States in every important aspect.

A precedent for the United States action can be found in the reservations to the proposed Senate resolution (never adopted) for the ratification of the treaty of Versailles. The fourth reservation to that resolution provided that "The United States reserves to itself exclusively the right to decide what questions are within its domestic jurisdiction...." [5]

Although the domestic jurisdiction reservation in the United States acceptance to the Optional Clause received such scant discussion in the Senate that one author said that the principal support for it "was mustered by a mere waving of the flag," [6] there was enough to show that the Senators intended to prevent the United States from being brought before the Court against its will. Senator Tom Connally, who introduced the amendment which provided for United States determination of domestic jurisdiction, argued that it was necessary because the Court might rule that a matter which was really domestic was not a domestic question. He said he had no intention of allowing a "Court of 15, 14 of whom will be alien judges... to decide that a domestic question is an

[2] The Charter reservation is silent on this point, but United Nations organs have always assumed this prerogative.

[3] *Congressional Record,* vol. 92, p. 10706.

[4] *United Nations Treaty Series,* vol. 1, p. 10.

[5] *Congressional Record,* vol. 59, p. 4599.

[6] Manley O. Hudson, "The Common Interpretation of the Mandates of International Law," *Proceedings of the American Society of International Law,* 1951, p. 49.

international question." On his fear with respect to the domestic affairs of the United States, he said:

...the United States is the object of envy of many nations of the world and many peoples. Our Treasury is most attractive to them. Immigration to our shores is something they dream of. I do not favor and I shall not vote to make it possible for the International Court of Justice to decide whether a question of immigration to our shores is a domestic question or an international question. It is a domestic question, of course; but the Court might contend it is international in character. The Court might say, "A man leaves one country and migrates to another, and therefore an international question is involved, and suit may be brought against the United States because it discriminates against the citizens of a certain country by not giving them a sufficiently large quota." [7]

The Connally amendment has aroused a considerable amount of comment. Since it is abundantly clear that the intention of the Senate was to reserve to the United States the competence to determine its own competence when a question of domestic jurisdiction arose, the early comment on the Connally amendment was not concerned with whether that was the intention of the Senate, but with what might happen in the event that the United States entered a plea of domestic jurisdiction in a case before the Court.

The ineffectiveness of Connally-type domestic jurisdiction reservations was demonstrated when the reservations of France [8] and the United States were brought before the International Court of Justice in the *Norwegian Loans* case [9] and the *Interhandel* case.[10] When Norway asked for reciprocal application of the reservation of France in a case in which France was suing Norway, the court held that there was no common will of the parties to confer jurisdiction on it and dismissed the case. In the *Interhandel* case the United States raised its own reservation (but it relied primarily on its local remedies objection) to bar a suit brought by Switzerland. The Court found the domestic jurisdiction reservation of the United States, as invoked, restricted and maintained by the United States, no bar to its jurisdiction.[11] These cases show that

[7] *Congressional Record,* vol. 92, p. 10695.

[8] France reserved "disputes relating to matters which are essentially within the national jurisdiction as understood by the Government of the French Republic." *United Nations Treaty Series,* vol. 26, p. 93.

[9] I.C.J. Rep. (1947), p. 9.

[10] I.C.J. Rep. (1959), p. 6.

[11] Herbert W. Briggs, "Interhandel: The Court's Judgment of March 21, 1959, on the Preliminary Objections of the United States," *American Journal of International Law,* vol. 53 (1959), pp. 547-563.

the domestic jurisdiction reservation is ineffective when international agencies (whether with a legal or political orientation) are specifically granted the competence to determine the question of their competence and that it is doubly ineffective when the reserving state specifically denies that competence to the international organ. It has the practical effect of barring claims that reserving states bring (if the defendant chooses to raise the claiming state's reservation) without protecting those states when claims are made against them (by a state that has not included a similar self-serving reservation in its acceptance of jurisdiction).

India replaced its declaration of acceptance of the Optional Clause which included a domestic jurisdiction reservation that did not claim final authority for India with a Connally-type reservation in January, 1956, after Portugal initiated the *Right of Passage over Indian Territory* case. A year later the Indian government terminated its acceptance of Optional Clause jurisdiction and did not reestablish it until January, 1960, at which time it reserved domestic matters without claiming a right of unilateral determination.[12]

The United Kingdom, apparently fearful that its nuclear testing program might be involved in a case in which the Court might issue interim orders of protection pending the determination of the jurisdictional question, deposited, in 1957, a national security reservation which left the determination of national security to the United Kingdom.[13] With some looseness of application, such a national security reservation could accomplish the same protection as the United States reservation.[14] The United Kingdom government rescinded the reservation in November, 1958,[15] and returned to the form of domestic jurisdiction reservation devised during the League period.

Following the use of the French reservation by Norway to block the case brought to the Court by France, the French government, in

[12] I.C.J. *Yearbook* (1959-60), pp. 241-242.

[13] *Ibid.*, (1957-58), p. 211.

[14] When asked during the debate on the Queen's speech whether he thought the new British reservation would cover the same area as the United States reservation, the Foreign Secretary answered rather ambiguously, but later added: "It seems to me that one must preserve the essential rights of his country.... I maintain that if we exercice our rights, our proceedings should not be subject to the jurisdiction of the International Court unless everybody accepts the same jurisdiction." *Parliamentary Debates*, 5th Ser., House of Commons, vol. 577, cols. 475-476 (Nov. 8, 1957).

[15] I.C.J. *Yearbook* (1958-59), pp. 225-226.

July 1959, replaced its reservation with one that left the determination of domestic jurisdiction to the Court.[16] The United States Government has not followed this example.

Admittedly, the issue of the "self-serving" reservation was not raised firmly or answered firmly in the *Interhandel* case. But Herbert W. Briggs suggested after this decision that

> the court may well have believed that the course of judicial statesmanship lay in treating the determination of domestic jurisdiction actually made by the United States under its reservation as no bar to the Court's jurisdiction, while leaving it to the United States to worry whether the Connally reservation is not more dangerous to United States interests than protective thereof.[17]

This conclusion led Briggs to call for withdrawal of the Connally amendment reservation,[18] but the spirit of nationalism which it exemplifies dies slowly in the United States. Nevertheless, the failure of the United States government to respond to this call does not revitalize the force of the reservation in the Courts. To hold open the possibility of national determination of international jurisdiction is to invite some future case in which the issue will be more carefully joined before the Court. The likelihood of United States defeat in such a venture suggests that a quiet burial is in order.

NONCOMPLIANCE WHEN RESERVATIONS FAIL

The minor successes of the League of Nations during its early years have often been noted.[19] During the same period the League met with some success in obtaining peaceful solutions to disputes in which a plea of domestic jurisdiction was raised. States that had objected to international organization interference on the basis of domestic jurisdiction nevertheless complied when they lost their cases.[20]

[16] *Ibid.*, p. 212.

[17] "Interhandel: The Court's Judgment of March 21, 1959, on the Preliminary Objections of the United States," 53 *American Journal of International Law*, 559 (1959).

[18] *Loc. cit.*, p. 563.

[19] See for example, Amry Vandenbosch and Willard N. Hogan, *The United Nations*, (New York: McGraw Hill Book Company, 1952), pp. 68-74.

[20] The League record, however, was not perfect. The international organization met defiance in the dispute between Finland and Russia (a nonmember) over Eastern Carelia. Russia claimed that the autonomy of the area was within its domestic jurisdiction. When the Council requested an advisory opinion from the Court and the Court notified the parties to the dispute that they might submit information on

When the Permanent Court of International Justice advised that the question of the Tunis-Morocco Nationality Decrees was not a domestic matter, the agent of the French Government announced that his country was prepared to submit the merits of the dispute to the Court. Before the case was argued, however, the dispute ended with an exchange of notes between the British Foreign office and the French ambassador in England. Without specifically referring to domestic jurisdiction, these notes provided that British nationals up to and including the second generation might decline French nationality. The notes did mention that neither side abandoned the points of view maintained at the Hague and that the agreement applied only in Tunis.[21]

An earlier domestic jurisdiction case, between Finland and Sweden over the Aaland Islands, was brought before the Council prior to the establishment of the Court. When Finland claimed domestic jurisdiction, the Council established a Committee of Jurists to advise it. The Committee ruled that the question was not domestic and, with the advice of a Committee of Rapporteurs, the Council adopted a resolution recognizing the sovereignty of Finland over the Aalands, but guaranteeing partial autonomy to the Islanders and directing the demilitarization of the area.[22] The plea of domestic jurisdiction did not prevent an outside settlement, but the recommendations were such that Finland could hardly be expected to deny the competence of the Council. Noting the final conclusion that Finland's sovereignty extended to the Aalands "leads logically to the conclusion that the question is an internal Finnish one," the delegate

the case, the Russian Commissar for Foreign Affairs refused to take part in the proceedings, claiming that his Government "absolutely repudiated the claim of the so-called League of Nations to intervene in the question of the internal affairs of Carelia." He further stated that "any attempt on the part of any power to apply to Russia the articles of the Covenant of the League relating to disputes between one of its members and a non-participating state would be regarded by the Russian Government as an act of hostility to the Russian State." Finland continued to press its claim in the League Assembly which resolved in 1923 that the question was "a matter of international concern, coming within the sphere of activity of the League of Nations." Nevertheless, for all practical purposes the defiance of Russia was successful. See *Official Journal,* Special Supplement No. 13, 1923, p. 48; John Bassett Moore, *International Law and Some Current Illusions* (New York: The Macmillan Company, 1924), p. 126.

[21] Cecil J. B. Hurst, "Interpretation of Article 15, Paragraph 8, of the Convenant of the League of Nations; Matters Solely Within the Jurisdiction of a State," *British Yearbook of International Law,* vol. 4 (1923-24), p. 178.

[22] *Official Journal,* September, 1921, p. 699.

of Finland added that the Finnish Government "did not wish to refuse to consider the suggestions made by the Rapporteurs." [23]

In the dispute between Greece and Turkey over the expulsion of the Oecumenical patriarch, Turkey (a nonmember) claimed domestic jurisdiction but participated in the early stage of the proceedings. The case arose from the exchange of minorities under a convention signed at Lausanne in 1923. The main point of the case turned on the meaning of the word "established," for certain persons established in Turkey were not to be included in the exchange. Although the case became aggravated, the League finally dropped the matter because Turkey and Greece settled the matter by bilateral negotiations.[24]

After 1930, the will to settle disputes peacefully and to accept obligations recommended for that purpose diminished. In those declining years of the League, only one major case which can in any way be classed as domestic came before the League, the problem of the Spanish Civil War. Although the Spanish Government appealed to the League, protesting the intervention of Germany and Italy in Spanish internal affairs, it also constantly reminded the League that the civil war was a matter of domestic jurisdiction.[25] In any event, by that time there was no collective will to deal with the question, for the League was slated to founder on this case long before it took it up.

Resistance to United Nations resolutions which have been preceded by a domestic jurisdiction plea have been common from the beginning of the United Nations. As is the case in any major international development, the causes for this are multiple, elusive, and subject to scholarly dispute. It is possible that a more experienced world community refused to repeat the illusion, held in the early days of the League, that international peace and security could be maintained through the collective security arrangements of an international organization. Considering the rising momentum for change and the increasing spirit of nationalism in the early years of the United Nations, doubts as to the viability of the new organization were immediately expressed. A member (or nonmember) might reasonably predict that noncompliance would be success-

[23] *Ibid.*, p. 704.

[24] For details see Manley O. Hudson, *The Permanent Court of International Justice* (New York: The MacMillan Company, 1932), pp. 186-189; *Official Journal,* April, 1925, pp. 441-442, 482-483, 488, 579-581; *Official Journal,* July, 1925, p. 1489.

[25] *Official Journal,* No. 1, January, 1937, pp. 8-10, 19; *Ibid.,* Nos. 5-6, May-June, 1937, p. 327.

ful and consequently refrain from complying until it was clear that others would accept their United Nations obligations. But the most direct cause is probably the one mentioned earlier; that is, decision-making majorities have interpreted an ambiguous Charter to impose new international obligations rather than to curtail them. An expanding membership has accelerated this development.

At first consideration, it might appear that the early League disputes over territory were of more vital interest to nations than many of the United Nations cases and that nations would, with justification, have been more reluctant to comply in those earlier cases than in the more recent ones. But in the assessment of matters which they want to handle with discretion, government officials more jealously guard their regulation of the entire citizenry than their right to pursue (without outside interference) policies that result in the induction into military service of a few persons with a dual citizenship or the control of a fragment of territory. The relative lack of interest in the United States over the recent territorial concessions to Mexico in the settlement of the old *Chamizal* case and the public furor that can be raised over the policies of the United States national government to end racial discrimination in the States (of the United States) give one a better perspective on the reaction of a government (and the general public of a member of the United Nations) when *an international organization* makes recommendations from *outside* regarding racial policies.

Certainly the delegates at the San Francisco conference were aware that allowing international organizations to bypass a national government and to deal directly with the people and to administer the affairs of the country (as in the Congo crisis) was a greater encroachment on state discretion than is an arrangement which brings another subject matter within the jurisdiction of an international organization for the purposes of discussion and recommendation.

In this perspective, it is not surprising that United Nations efforts to undermine the Franco regime in Spain did not foment a revolution in that country or elicit support from all members. A two-part resolution called upon members to recall from Madrid their ambassadors and ministers plenipotentiary and barred the Franco Government in Spain from membership in international agencies associated with the United Nations. Three states recalled their ambassadors or ministers; nineteen had no ambassador or minister accredited to Spain at that time; thirty had no diplomatic relations with Spain. To the initial survey of compliance by the Secretary-General, Liberia replied that she would comply, the

Dominican Republic promised proper consideration, and Argentina simply acknowledged receipt of the communication.[26] The Franco regime remained in power, and was eventually admitted to the United Nations. The initial objections of the international community have almost faded from memory.

South Africans complain that their domestic jurisdiction has been violated by the United Nations organs without responding to calls for change in their racial policies. Even with the efforts to employ measures under Chapter VII of the Charter to increase the pressure on the Smith Government in Rhodesia, the "illegal racist minority regime" has survived since November 11, 1965. National government protests that United Nations peacekeeping forces violated domestic jurisdiction in the Congo are an exception, but in this instance, the protest came after the introduction of United Nations forces and was a temporary complaint by a regime that was hardly able to maintain itself.

In summary, although a plea of domestic jurisdiction is usually ineffective to prevent the passage of resolutions that call for national action in allegedly domestic cases, a state may, if it wishes to go beyond orderly processes of avoidance within the organization, succeed when it does not comply with those obligations.

PROTECTION OF DOMESTIC JURISDICTION BY WALKOUTS

Although walkouts now are limited to an occasional exercise during one speech, apparently to emphasize diplomatic displeasures,[27] at one time they promised to become a successful device to express extreme opposition to passage of resolutions (in the face of domestic jurisdiction pleas) that would pressure the international organization into rescinding the obligation as a means of bringing the recalcitrant state back to active participation in other international organization activities. Because an expansion in membership since that date could result in an increased

[26] G.A.O.R., 2nd Sess., Supplement No. 1, Annual Report of the Secretary General (1947), p. 3.

[27] This discussion of walkouts does not relate to resolutions or situations in which a domestic jurisdiction plea is not involved. When the Soviet delegate boycotted the Security Council in protest to the seating of the delegate of Nationalist China, the absence was not related to domestic jurisdiction. The cases covered here lasted longer than one speech and were in protest to United Nations refusal to accept a domestic jurisdiction plea.

tendency to intervene which could, in turn, cause a return of such practices, it seems worthwhile to examine briefly the nature of this technique and the degree of its success.

During its 1955 session, the General Assembly dealt with two cases involving France (the Algerian question and the Moroccan question) and two involving South Africa (the treatment of Indians in South Africa and the question of race conflict in South Africa resulting from policies of *apartheid*). France and South Africa walked out in connection with the Algerian question and the *apartheid* question.

Although neither walkout constituted complete withdrawal from the United Nations, the French action was more extreme. The French boycott extended to most United Nations organs. The South African delegation stated an intention to be absent only when the racial policies of South Africa were discussed, but reserved the right to return to vote on the question.

Until the French and South African walkouts, less vigorous protests of domestic jurisdiction during debate had been ineffective,[28] but the French and South African walkouts temporarily accomplished their goals. The General Assembly dropped the Algerian item from its agenda by a unanimous vote.[29] In the explanation of votes that followed, some of the delegates called attention to the necessity of French participation during the forthcoming Assembly debate on disarmament.[30] The Assembly retained the *apartheid* question on the agenda but rejected the major portion of the draft resolution of that session. Besides disposing of the question for that session, the Assembly discontinued the special commission on the racial question in South Africa and rejected a proposal to retain the item on the agenda for the next year.[31]

Following the Assembly's decisions, a *New York Times* editorial writer concluded that the Assembly "presumably will refrain in the future

[28] For example, when the Indonesian question was before the Security Council, the delegate of the Netherlands repeatedly protested that the matter was domestic, but he continued to participate in the debates and his Government did not refuse to honor the Council's orders. Regarding the Council's cease-fire order (which he called an "invitation") he said that his Government accepted the "Council's wish that military action should cease, not because it recognized the Council's jurisdiction, which it expressly did not, but because it wanted to take into full account the humanitarian motives which no doubt were the foundation of the Council's action," S.C.O.R., 2nd Year, No. 77, p. 2012.

[29] G.A.O.R., 10th Sess., Plenary Meetings, p. 371.

[30] *Ibid.*, 10th Sess., Plenary Meetings, pp. 371-381.

[31] *Ibid.*, 10th Sess., Plenary Meetings, p. 404.

from intervening in situations which, however distressing, are not properly matters for international action." [32]

As is now well known, these were temporary respites. The General Assembly resumed discussion of Algeria and that country later was separated from France, the latter responding as much to local Algerian pressures as to those of the world community. As the newly-independent states of Africa have joined the United Nations, the debate on South Africa has become even more acrimonious. At this time, it does not appear likely that a South African walkout would intimidate the present majority in the United Nations.

During the Hungarian crises of 1956, the delegate of that country walked out [33] and Soviet support of the new Hungarian government stymied international action. Apparently walkouts supported by an adamant major power and capable of being countermanded only by an intrusion of United Nations forces against the will of local authorities can be effective. But this success is due more to the physical strength of the major power than to the technique of the walkout.[34]

If resolutions in the face of domestic jurisdiction pleas could not be so easily disregarded, walkouts might have developed as a common practice. As it is, noncompliance after passage of resolutions causes less furor than walkouts and recalcitrant states amass less ill will by the quieter method. If resolutions achieve more force, walkouts could return to use.

[32] December 18, 1955, Section 4, p. 6.

[33] *New York Times,* December 12, 1956, p. 1.

[34] A similar example of major power support can be seen in the Czechoslovak *coup d'état* of 1948, although the Czechoslovak refusal to participate was more a "changing of the guard" than a walkout. After the Czech delegate asked for an investigation of the *coup,* he was removed by the new government which appointed his successor but declined to discuss a matter it classed as domestic. The matter was dropped rather quickly in the Security Council after the Soviet Union, by the use of a "double" veto, forced a resolution to investigate the matter into the substantive category and then vetoed it. S.C.O.R., Third Year. Supplement for April, p. 6; *Ibid.,* Third Year, No. 56, pp. 2-14, 19, 26, 32.

CHAPTER VIII

THE MIDDLE EAST CASE

INTRODUCTION

Basically, there are two contradictory views of the belligerents in the many-faceted contest in the Middle East:

> On the Arab side, there is the prescriptive right to a land inhabited for more than a thousand years, the right of self-determination, the shock to the dignity of a once great people, the fear of Israeli expansionism, the plight of one million refugees. On the Israeli side, there is the undissolved and indissoluble bond to the land which had been the cradle of the Jewish heritage, the urge of Jews barred from the nations of Europe to reconstruct a national life of their own in the land of their ancestors, their need for a refuge among brethren when all other havens were denied, and their internationally recognized right to a share of Palestine.[1]

These "insoluble" and antithetic positions of the two groups have been a constant shadow since the conclusion of World War II and the formal creation of the state of Israel immediately following. Yet, this is but a modern version of the conflict which dates back to the history of mankind itself. It is not the purpose of this study to undertake a complete historical study. What is attempted here is a documentation and study of a small portion of the contemporary conflict between Israel and her Arab neighbors and of the political issues and legal ramifications surrounding the conflict with emphasis on the denunciation of or noncompliance with United Nations actions.

It must be recalled from the outset that since the creation of the state of Israel on May 15, 1948, no less than three wars have been fought, and the threat of an expanded global contest has been a real possibility, especially since the Suez crisis of 1956. Basically, the first confrontation of 1948-49 was, in legal terms, a contest over "sovereignty, territory and

[1] Nadav Safran, "The Arab-Israeli Dispute in Perspective," *Current History*, vol. 53, no. 316 (1967), p. 321.

property rights." And for Israel, psychologically, the contest was over the issue of fulfilling "a Biblical promise of the 'land of Canaan' as 'an everlasting possession.' " For Arabs, it was a case of "unlawful" seizure of land (Palestine) which had been the home for Arabs for more than a thousand years and the implicit threat of Israeli expansionism at their expense. Nor can Arabs easily overlook the some six million Jewish people in the United States.

Upon reflection, at the time of the Suez crisis the dimension of conflict suddenly took on a much more intense global implication than it had at the time of the 1948-49 conflict. At least two things, among others, appear as readily noticeable historical milestones which are related to this abrupt turn of events: (1) circumstances surrounding the Aswan Dam, and (2) the general Soviet "offensive" in the Middle East. These two considerations are admittedly related.

To begin with, notice should be made of the first, though short-lived, confrontation between Israel and her Arab neighbors which ended with an armistice agreement (1949) and which, among other things, prompted the Western powers (the United States, Great Britain, and France) to declare (1950) "their opposition to the development of an arms race between the Arab and Israel" as, undoubtedly, a precautionary measure for the recurrence of conflict between the hostile neighbors. Since then, the newly established revolutionary regime in Egypt headed by a military leader, Gamal Abdel Nasser, felt the weight of Western reluctance or refusal to assist with necessary arms for Egyptian security especially in view of the hostile Israel, and slowly began to turn elsewhere for arms (i.e., the Soviet bloc). Perhaps because of the obvious implication of the Soviet arms assistance to the Cairo government, the United States government and the United Kingdom in 1955 showed a new interest in assisting (some seventy million dollars worth) in the Egyptian government's intense commitment for the Aswan Dam project. By then, it seems, the Soviet influence in the area had been too well established for the turn to be reversed.

Nasser had by then made an almost complete about-face from the United States by, for instance, recognizing continental China, securing final evacuation of the British troops from the Canal zone, and receiving military aid from the communist bloc countries. Infuriated by these Egyptian moves, the Washington government in 1956 withdrew its earlier promise to assist in the construction of the Aswan Dam. Nasser took it as a "slap in the face."

The 1956 confrontation, it appears, was a confrontation at two levels. On the one level, it was a maneuver of big powers: the United States' commitment to the "containment policy" and the Soviet Union's anxiety to change the balance of power in the Middle East; on the second level, it was the immediate confrontation between the hostile neighbors.

The 1956 contest was prompted by Nasser's decision to nationalize the Suez Canal. The Western Big Three objected to the move, which was in turn followed by a contest between the Israeli armed forces and those of Egypt on October 29, 1956. Two days later, Anglo-French forces began attacking Egyptian airfields and ultimately landed paratroops in the canal zone. While the United States government refused to be "involved" in the contest, the Soviet Union had declared its willingness to send "volunteers" to Egypt.

The contest was finally, if only temporarily, terminated by the actions of the United Nations General Assembly in two resolutions: the first ordered withdrawal of the Anglo-French forces from Egypt and the pull-back of the Israeli forces from the Gaza strip and the Gulf of Aqaba to the 1949 Armistice line; the second resolution provided for sending a United Nations Emergency Force to police the troubled area.

The direction by this time was toward a seemingly irreversible arms race. J. C. Hurewitz finds that:

> The value of military imports to the Middle East from all external sources jumped from perhaps $2.0 billion in the first postwar decade to $9.25 billion in the second, and the pace was still quickening at the start of the third, for the retail value of arms exported to the Middle East from all external sources exceeded $1.5 billion each year in 1966 and 1967.[2]

In addition, he finds that:

> The United States became the region's paramount supplier in the second postwar decade, sending to its thirteen clients from Morocco to Afghanistan and Pakistan probably as much as $5.5 billion worth of modern arms, and to this its major allies (Britain, France, and West Germany) may have added another Billion dollars worth. The U.S.S.R. ran second, funneling to six Middle East countries weapons with a market value of more than $2.25 billion, and when shipments from Czechoslovakia (and, one marginal scale, Poland) are included, the total value of arms reaching the region from the Communist bloc was raised by another $0.5 billion.
> A closer look at the gross statistics reveals that more than 75 per cent of Western (mostly American) regional military aid was destined for three countries: Turkey,

[2] J. C. Hurewitz, *Middle East Politics: The Military Dimension,* (New York: Frederick A. Praeger, 1969), p. 439.

Iran, and Pakistan, all of them members of CENTO, the "northern tier" alliance.... In contrast, 80 per cent of Soviet (and Czech) military aid to the Middle East in the second postwar decade went to three Arab countries: Egypt, Syria, and Iraq. ...Altogether, the U.S.S.R. and Czechoslovakia pumped into the three Arab countries in a single decade military hardware that would probably have been priced in the market at more than $2.2 billion.[3]

Aside from the conventional political bases of "containment" and the maintenance of the political status quo in the area, the United States and, therefore, the Soviet Union have more immediate military rationale for their competition in the area. According to one military authority:

1. Its location is the prime factor. The Middle East lies at a strategic crossroads between Europe, Africa and Asia. This should not be viewed in the outmoded contest of overland movements by ancient Babylonian armies. Today's Middle East is a tremendous complex of land, sea and air routes—and communications.
2. The area also has enormous riches in the form of huge oil reserves, vitally needed in the modern world.
3. Ever since Czarist days, Russia's leaders have coveted the mideast because of its location. Present Soviet rulers...covet the area even more strongly.
4. The masses of people of the Mideast, and therefore their control, are another vital factor in overall strategic balance.
5. In its new manifestations, the Middle East is developing what might be called a "strategic reach," which extends its importance beyond the immediate area.[4]

Whatever validity one may attach to the foregoing analysis, it is difficult to ignore the importance of the Middle East as a focal point of contest between the two giants for influence. As though history had foreseen the importance of the area, the Middle East has been a "first" in many of the United Nations forums:

one of the first items to go before the Security Council...was a complaint by a Middle East country, Iran, against the Soviet interference in Iranian internal matters, as a result of which in May 1946 all Soviet troops were withdrawn from Iranian territory.
The first Special Session of the UN General Assembly, in April-May 1947, was devoted to seeking a satisfactory plan for the future of Palestine.
The first vote on the disposition of a territory—Palestine—was taken by the General Assembly in November 1947, when it approved the partition of Palestine into separate Jewish and Arab states, linked by an economic union, with Jerusalem as an international city.

[3] *Ibid.*, pp. 439-441.

[4] (Maj. Gen.) Max S. Johnson, U.S. Army (Ret.), "U.S. Stake in the Mideast," *U.S. News and World Report,* June 19, 1967, p. 37.

The first Emergency Special Session of the General Assembly, held in November 1956, was convened to consider the Suez crisis.
The first international peace force—the Emergency Force—was created by the UN General Assembly, after the Suez fighting in 1956, to patrol the borders between Israel and Egypt.
The first truce arranged by the UN was that between Israel and some of the Arab states in 1948.[5]

It is, therefore, correct to say that "the Arab-Israeli war of 1967 did not so much create new policy problems...as underscore a great many existing ones." It must also be recalled that by the time the third and the most recent war had begun, the East-West arms race in the region had already taken a definite shape; hence, no solution seemed possible for the problem without a part accorded to the great powers. It must also be recalled that in the three open contests between Arabs and Israelis, the latter have been able not only to maintain themselves but also to extend significantly control over the Arab territories. The latest contest in 1967 "fruited" some four times as large a territory as its original size.

RECALCITRANCE DURING THE SUEZ CRISIS

To the Arabs, and to the Israelis as well, the storied virtues of settlement by compromise seem an alien goal, for the basis of the contest allegedly is not, and has not been, subject to negotiation. To the Arabs, existence of the Jewish state of Israel in Arab territory is not, and has never been, acceptable either in law or in fact. The displacement of countless Palestinian refugees from their homeland and their ensuing hardships are the basis of Arab determination to "right the wrong."

In the language of politics, this determination means nonrecognition of the Israeli government, and the promise for eventual recovery of the land occupied by the Jewish state. In this mission, political and religious destinies of the Arab states are in agreement. In the terms of "real politik," the political destiny of Arab states has meaning only if it promises "eventual recovery" of the lost land, and toward this end,

[5] *INTERCOM,* (New York: Foreign Policy Association, Inc., 1967), vol. 9, no. 6 (1967), p. 39; see also M. H. el-Farra, "Role of the United Nations vis-a-vis the Palestine Question," *Law and Contemporary Problems,* vol. 33 (1968), pp. 68-77; For the texts of resolutions passed by the Security Council and the General Assembly on the Middle East Question, see *Middle East Journal,* vol. 21 (1967), pp. 396-398.

leaders of the Arab world are bound, whatever may be the expense, to uphold and promote the demands of their people, real or imagined, *vis-a-vis* Israel.

This inflexibility of the Arab stand can be matched only by the Israeli determination to survive in the midst of hostile neighbors. Israeli survival has special meaning, not only because of its peoples' experience during World War II, but also because of its real or imagined repossession of, if not reincarnation in, the land of its ancestors. To the Jews, the state of Israel is, though meager in size, the very essence of being Jewish, for the long-lost Jewish state has finally founded a seat. What is intentionally suggested here by the omission of apparent claims and counterclaims of a more immediate political nature is the importance of more fundamental considerations, most of which are, as stated previously, allegedly not subject to compromise or negotiation.

The initial Israeli defiance of United Nations' actions was manifested in its reluctance to implement the call for withdrawal of forces at the time of the Suez crisis of 1956. Although compliance was finally accomplished and United Nations forces to police the cease fire were admitted, United Nations members were, at that time, obviously fearful that the defiance would become complete and that Israel would, by its recalcitrance, increase its responsibility for the situation.

Discussion of the Suez crisis began in the Security Council but, because of the disagreement among the permanent members, it was transferred to the General Assembly, which based its activity on the "uniting for peace" resolution. In the deployment of forces on Egyptian territory and the territory under the military control of Israel, no advances were made without the consent of the government concerned.

In a White House statement immediately after the Israeli troops entered the Sinai peninsula, President Eisenhower announced that the United States would bring the matter before the Security Council and recalled that his country had pledged itself to assist the victim of any "aggression" in the Middle East.[6] However, the United States letter requesting a special meeting of the Council to consider the problem referred to the "military action of Israel in Egypt." [7] In the Security Council, the United States delegate used this same language when he called for prompt Council determination that "a breach of the peace has

[6] *New York Times,* October 30, 1956, p. 1.

[7] U.N. Doc. S/3706.

occurred and to make clear...that the Israel armed forces should be immediately withdrawn behind the established armistice lines." [8] Although the draft resolution of the United States delegation included no reference to a breach of the peace or an act of aggression, it implied strongly the responsibility of Israel.[9] This implication is buttressed by the United States delegate's reaction to a proposed new paragraph, suggested by several members, which would have called upon *both* Israel and Egypt immediately to cease fire. He said that he would accept it, but did not think it necessary. Later, in the House of Commons, Prime Minister Eden said the United States resolution "was in effect a condemnation of Israel as the aggressor." [10]

In the Security Council debates, Egypt called the action "armed aggression." Israel denied the charge, replying that it was the victim, not the author, of aggression.[11] The Soviet and Yugoslav delegates declared Israel the aggressor and the Soviet delegate noted the absence from the United States draft resolution of "a vitally important clause, one whereby the Council would condemn Israel for its aggression." [12] Following the vetoes of this resolution and the subsequent Soviet resolution, the matter was transferred to the General Assembly, where, in the light of the British and French entry into the conflict, the nature of their acts was also brought into question.

[8] S.C.O.R., 11th Year, 748th Meeting, pp. 1-2.

[9] The text of the resolution as introduced: "*Noting* that the armed forces of Israel have penetrated deeply into Egyptian territory in violation of the General Armistice Agreement between Egypt and Israel; *Expressing its grave concern* at this violation of the Armistice Agreement: 1. *Calls upon* Israel immediately to withdraw its armed forces behind the established armistice lines. 2. *Calls upon* all Members (a) To refrain from the use of force or threat of force in the area in any manner inconsistent with the purposes of the United Nations; (b) To assist the United Nations in ensuring the integrity of the Armistice Agreements; (c) To refrain from giving any military, economic or financial assistance to Israel so long as it has not complied with this resolution. 3. Requests the Secretary-General to keep the Security Council informed on compliance with this resolution and to make whatever recommendations he deems appropriate for the maintenance of international peace and security in the area by the implementation of this and prior resolutions." An additional operative paragraph calling upon Israel and Egypt immediately to cease fire was accepted by the United States. U.N. Doc. S/3710; amended version quoted S.C.O.R., 11th Year, 749th Meeting, p. 31.

[10] *New York Times,* November 1, 1956, p. 20.

[11] S.C.O.R., 11th Year, 749th Meeting, p. 18.

[12] *Ibid.,* 11th Year, 748th Meeting, pp. 4-5; 749th Meeting, p. 8. The Soviet delegate nevertheless supported the United States resolution.

In the General Assembly, the pattern remained about the same. The Egyptian delegate and about two dozen others either called the action aggression or strongly implied the responsibility of Israel, Britain or France. Nevertheless, a large majority of the speakers supported the United States resolution, which again stopped short of calling the actions aggression,[13] and the resolution was adopted by a vote of sixty-four to five with six abstentions. The delegates of the Soviet bloc and the Afro-Asian bloc generally referred to the action as aggression; Israel, Britain and France denied the charge; the remainder avoided a statement on that point.

Undoubtedly, the determination of the responsible party or parties would have been difficult in the Suez crisis. Actions must be assessed in the light of the situation in which they were taken and their motivation, but as the Assembly, in the course of Israel's delay on withdrawal, recalled its previous resolutions on cease-fire and withdrawal, there were many statements deploring Israeli recalcitrance and several representatives warned that noncompliance constituted an extension of the original aggression. This development called attention to the practice that developed during the League of Nations period for fixing responsibility without taking a formal vote to name the aggressor.

In Article 10 of the Covenant of the League of Nations, the Members undertook "to respect and preserve as against external aggression the territorial integrity and existing political independence of all Members of the League." "Aggression" was not defined, but in Article 16 there was provision that any Member that resorted to war in disregard of its covenants under Articles 12, 13 and 15 would "*ipso facto* be deemed to have committed an act of war." During the League period some attempts were made to determine responsibility for breaches of the peace by assembling evidence "concerning priority in initiating hostilities, aggressive intentions, and superiority of preparation for attack," but the "concept of provisional orders" implied in the above-quoted Articles of the Covenant "came to dominate League thinking." [14] By this latter formula,

[13] The resolution provided: "*Nothing*... that the armed forces of Israel have penetrated deeply into Egyptian territory in violation of the General Armistice Agreement between Egypt and Israel..., *Nothing* that armed forces of France and the United Kingdom of Great Britain and Northern Ireland are conducting military operations against Egyptian territory... 1. Urges... that all parties... agree to an immediate cease fire." Resolution 997 (ES-1) G.A.O.R., 1st ESS, p. 11.

[14] Quincy Wright, "The Prevention of Aggression," *American Journal of International Law,* vol. 50 (1956), pp. 520-521.

it was not necessary to make an examination on the merits to determine an aggressor. Once a breach of the peace occurred, the League organ issued a cease-fire order and the party which failed to obey branded itself as the aggressor.[15]

Despite its frustration, the majority in the General Assembly was unwilling to make the assumption that is involved in the "provisional orders method." As is well known, affirmative determinations citing Article 39 have been exceptional, and only in the Korean case has aggression been determined. This determination was by the General Assembly in its resolution of February 1, 1951. In other cases, no United Nations organ has gone further than determining the nature of the situation and ordering provisional measures.[16] In the Middle East case, the President of the United States could speak of applying the law to friend and foe alike, but that could hardly lead to his joining the Soviet Union in declaring any of the parties in the Suez crisis an aggressor, either by a formal vote or by a conclusion that by its delay Israel brought the responsibility on itself.

The obvious conclusion is that in such crossfires of international politics as the Suez crisis, states may go far in delaying compliance to a General Assembly call for cease fire and withdrawal without suffering a penalty for such inaction.

THREATENED DEFIANCE SINCE 1967

A more dramatic case of Israeli defiance of United Nations' actions arose after the latest contest in 1967. In essence, Israeli defiance is stated in the following terms:

1. That Algeria, Syria and Iraq had publicly announced their rejection of the Security Council's cease-fire order at the conclusion of the six day war in June 1967;
2. That all fifteen member states of the Security Council (January 1969) maintain diplomatic relations with Arab nations but six of them refuse to maintain any ties with Israel; of these, Algeria is even in a formal state of war with Israel;
3. That, as the Israeli government sees it, there are at least eight automatic pro-Arab votes in the Council, while the remaining seven members do not

[15] *Ibid.* See also Willard N. Hogan, *International Conflict and Collective Security,* (Lexington: University of Kentucky Press, 1955), p. 53.

[16] For example, in the Indonesian question, the Security Council called upon the parties "to cease hostilities forthwith" and the parties accepted. S.C.O.R., 2nd Year, No. 68, pp. 1702, 1716-1717.

necessarily support the Israeli position; hence, the possibility of a pro-Israeli Council decision is inconceivable.[17]

Assuredly, the decision is based on Israeli pessimism over the objectivity of the pending Security Council decision,[18] and is also based on precedences of defiance. In fact, the Israeli defiance is not without practicable foundation, yet the fact of defiance to the dictates of the Organization can not be easily dismissed.

Most specifically, and as in all cases of noncompliance of defiance, the Charter stipulations on membership obligations, Chapters VI and VII, become immediately applicable. In the specific case of the Middle East contest, the following points form the bases of the most important issues: (1) right of existence and the state of war; (2) legal regime of a multinational gulf and territorial waters; (3) the question of "fruits of aggression."

Right of Existence and the State of War

Implicit in the Israeli denunciation of the Security Council decision is the question of the Israeli right of existence, and the threat thereto (real or imagined). On this point, it has to be conceded that the state of Israel has been recognized by all the principal powers of the world and by the the United Nations. However, she is not recognized by her neighbors in the Arab world, which have been at "war" with Israel

[17] For a description of Israeli announcement on this and related points, see *Christian Science Monitor,* January 25, 1969, p. 2.

[18] Of the many resolutions which were passed both by General Assembly and Security Council, the following are especially noteworthy: On June 6, 1967, at the outbreak of hostilities, the Security Council unanimously adopted a resolution [Resolution 233 (1967); S/7935] which called for an "immediate cease-fire and for a cessation of all military activities in the area." On June 11, 1967, the Council again adopted Resolution 236 (1967) [S/7930 and Add. 1] which ordered "prompt return to the cease-fire position." Subsequently, on June 14, 1967, the Council adopted Resolution 237 (1967 [S/7968/Rev. 1-3, orally amended by Mali] which ordered Israel to "ensure the safety, welfare and security of the inhabitants of the areas where military operations have taken place."

The most basic Council decision on the Middle East crisis was outlined on the Resolution 242 (1967) [S/8247] which was adopted on November 22, 1967, the substance of which states (1) "inadmissibility of the acquisition of territory by war"; (2) "withdrawal of Israel armed forces from territories occupied in the recent conflict"; (3) "(t)ermination of all claims or states of belligerency"; (4) "guaranteeing freedom of navigation through international waterways in the area"; (5) "a just settlement of the refugee problem", among others.

continuously since the earliest days of the Israeli proclamation of independence. While as a matter of general principle the act of recognition is solely a national decision, the state of war is not. In this connection, one of the related considerations in analyzing Arab-Israeli relations of recent years has been the question of belligerency, or the state of war: it has been consistently maintained by the Arab nations, especially Egypt (1) that its unilateral prohibition of Israeli use of the Suez Canal since the 1956 war, and later the use of the Gulf of Aqaba and the Strait of Tiran, was based on the right of belligerent states to undertake those measures essential for self-defense, and (2) that the blockades in question are consistent with laws governing relations of belligerent nations.

The contention goes further in stating that while the succession of armistice agreements has temporarily halted the actual military phase of the belligerency, the agreements in no way alter the legal or political state of war. Hence, applicable international law of war dictates that Israeli and Israeli-connected shipping through the national canal or strait is not and can not be construed within the legal norms applicable in time of peace, that is, Israeli and Israeli-connected shipping is not in a technical sense "innocent passage."

The counter arguments seem to stress (1) that both Israel and Egypt, as members of the United Nations, are duty bound to resolve their disputes through peaceful means in such a manner as not to endanger international peace and security (hence, rejection of a state of war which is unsanctioned either by the Security Council under Chapter VII or under Article 51 of the Charter) and (2) that the state of war as unilaterally claimed by Arab states is illegal and inapplicable. It is further argued that the succession of armistice agreements signed under the auspices of the United Nations denies a recurrence or resumption of any military operation, hence, even a *de facto* state of war can not be recognized without violating the dictates of the Charter.

A question arises, therefore, as to the precise meaning of an armistice. If in fact an armistice is a recognized legal instrument terminating war, the Arab (especially Egyptian) claim does not seem to have a valid legal foundation.

In this connection, traditional norms of international law seem to dictate that an armistice is not synonymous with a peace treaty; there seems to be little disagreement on this point. But problems occur concerning (1) the validity or recognizability of the state of war under contemporary international law and, (2) the seemingly changing concept of "armistice." As stated previously, the Charter and contemporary norms of international law deny emphatically the legal validity of a state of war; yet, a *de facto* state of war is acknowledgedly a common phenomenon in contemporary international relations. As for the changing concept of an "armistice," practices of the international community during the post World War II period indicate that while an armistice is technically a military arrangement for cessation of hostilities on a temporary basis (implicitly) without in any way altering the political status of belligerency, armistice has been used in actual practice as the principal instrument through which conflicts have been terminated and implicitly, also, on a permanent basis (the cases of armistice as a "new type of peace treaty," the illustrations of Korea and Indochina (especially in view of the still "hot" political and military contest in Vietnam, and a threat for one in Korea) do not suffice to allege a changed nature of the concept.

It is perhaps more fruitful to pursue a definition of armistice on the precepts of the Charter than to rely on a few isolated examples. If the spirit of the Charter were put into force in its absolutes, there would exist no question but that armistice in conflict with, or unsanctioned by, the United Nations decisions could not exist as a norm, for the possibility of war itself is denied.

Legal Regime of a Multinational Gulf and Territorial Waters[19]

The second point of major contest centers around the determination of the legal regime of the Gulf of Aqaba and Strait of Tiran. The Gulf of Aqaba, which became one of the main issues of the latest Arab-Israeli contest, in point of fact has the following dimensions:

> The Gulf of Aqaba is somewhat over one hundred miles in length, and varies in width between three miles on the narrow bay at its northern end and seventeen miles at its widest point. The mouth—from Sinai Peninsula headland to Arabian Peninsula headland—is approximately nine miles in width. A valve-shaped island at the entrance, however, Tiran Island, further narrows the possibility of access to the Gulf, and, in fact, creates two entrances thereto. The western and principal entrance passes between Tiran Island the Sinai Peninsula shore. It is approximately four miles in breadth, and has two channels, Enterprise Passage and Grafton

[19] For further analysis, see Charles B. Selak, Jr., "A Consideration of the Legal Status of the Gulf of Aqaba," *American Journal of International Law,* vol. 52 (1958), pp. 660-698; see also I. Blischenko, "International Law and the Middle East Crisis," *International Affairs,* (Moscow), January, 1969, pp. 29-35.

Passage. The former, which lies close to the Sinai Peninsula coast, is the principal shipping channel into the Gulf, and the only channel which can be navigated safely by vessels of substantial size.[20]

As a multinational gulf, it is bordered by four littoral states: (1) Egypt, (2) Saudi Arabia, (3) Jordan, and (4) Israel. Both Egypt and Saudi Arabia claimed six miles of territorial seas, plus an additional six miles as a contiguous zone; Jordan claimed "that part of the sea which is contiguous to the coast...and...three miles"; Israel claimed six miles.

From the foregoing, two points become apparent: (1) inasmuch as the Gulf is three miles at the narrowest point and seventeen miles at the widest point, national claims of littoral states come into conflict at certain points, and, conversely, there are portions of gulf which are outside the claimed national jurisdictions of the littoral states; (2) since Enterprise Passage provides the only safe access to the Gulf, and since the Passage is located within six miles of the territorial sea claimed by Egypt, vessels headed toward or coming from ports within the Gulf must transit the Egyptian territorial sea.

In this context, the legality of Egyptian control (e.g., blockade of Israeli and Israeli-connected shipping) is seemingly dependent upon: (1) determination of the status of the Gulf (that is, whether or not the Gulf is territorial or international in character), and (2) the right (or lack of the right) of innocent passage in the circumstances determined immediately above.

In general, the Arab claims for the Gulf as a territorial sea of the Arab nations are based on the concept of "historical gulf", as closed body of water, having been used exclusively by Arabs for centuries without external objections prior to the current contest. Hence, the claim of "innocent passage" for a belligerent nation (Israel) is inapplicable. The counterclaim, that of Israel, is that the Gulf is not a territorial sea, being a part of an open sea enclosed by more than one littoral state; hence, the right of innocent passage.

The example of the Black Sea and Turkish control or lack of control of the strait and the vessels of the littoral states (as well as those of other nations) in time of peace seems to indicate that the Egyptian blockade of Israeli shipping via the Strait of Tiran is based on shallow legal ground, but only if the alleged state of war between the belligerents is denied. On the other hand, the Gulf of Fonseca decision of the Central American Court of International Justice seems to conflict with the above stated;

[20] Selak, *op. cit.*, p. 660.

in that case, the Court found that the Gulf (which is surrounded by Nicaragua, Honduras, and El Salvador and is approximately equal in size and configuration to the Gulf of Aqaba) is a "historic bay," belonging to littoral states.

In this connection, while the two Geneva Conventions on the Territorial Sea and the Contiguous Zone, and on the High Seas (1958) have greatly facilitated the general principles governing territorial seas and related concepts (innocent passage, etc.) they failed to answer all questions, specifically pertaining to the Gulf of Aqaba.

The Question of "Fruits of Aggression"

An additional question of importance is that of retaining "fruits of aggression." Basically, this question can be addressed in several ways: Could a state under contemporary international law retain "fruits of aggression"? If not, could a state retain part of a foreign territory acquired as a result of war for the purpose of a final negotiated settlement? Could it, then, be justified as a measure of self-defense?

As for the first point, norms of contemporary international law seem emphatic in their condemnation of the practice of retaining "fruits of aggression," for, as stated previously, not only are states required to resolve their disputes peacefully but the very essence of war has been made devoid of legal status. Likewise, all members (as well as non-members) of the United Nations are required to resolve their disputes in such a manner as not to threaten or endanger international peace and security, and, in the event of failure to do so, the Security Council is empowered to impose sanction or otherwise recommend a mode of solution. Again, no dispute (either in fact or in law) which is not a matter falling either under the domestic jurisdiction clause of the Charter or under Article 51 is immune from the foregoing. Even in cases of "self-defense" (Article 51), measures undertaken by an individual state or collectivity of states are subject to the Security Council determination of fact and appropriate action; hence, limitations on the duration of action, and subsequent review.[21]

[21] For further discussion on the legal aspect of self-defense, see F. S. Lin, "Self-Defense—A Permissible Use of Force Under the U.N. Charter," *De Paul Law Review,* vol. 13 (1963), pp. 43-72. See also R. Higgins, "Legal Limits to the Use of Force by Sovereign States—United Nations Practice," *British Yearbook of International Law,* vol. 37 (1961), pp. 269-319; Hans Kelsen, *The Law of the United Nations,* (New York: Frederick A. Praeger, 1966), pp. 791-805.

Inasmuch as the status of war is "outlawed," and inasmuch as Arab territory currently is indisputably under Israeli control, an answer to the question of retaining "fruits of aggression" seems self-evident. The claim of "self-defense," while it is used reciprocally by belligerents on both sides as bases of their actions can not, it seems, form a basis for retaining occupied territory, especially in view of the continued and consistent Security Council resolutions to the contrary. Additionally, the argument for the necessity of retaining the occupied territories as a bargaining point in eventual negotiations (an argument of a "just end" through "means" which are questionable) is doubtful, for the norms of international law surely can not be based on the conflict of "means" and "ends."

Likewise, the Egyptian claim of a "state of war" is seemingly not so much a question of law as one of state of mind, for it appears undeniable that this claim has two pitfalls: (1) while the Egyptian government claims its nonrecognition of Israel, the claim of a "state of war" presumes (if not recognizes at least *de facto*) the existence of the state of Israel;[22] (2) the "state of war" as a basis of justification for military action is and has been long recognized as an obsolete, invalid legal claim. It appears doubtful, therefore, that a state can justify the legality of its action when the very legal norms upon which it relies deny the very activity in question.

CONCLUSIONS

Apparent from the foregoing discussions is the hopelessness of any meaningful and mutually satisfactory solution to the conflict, for the very concept of "justice" knows no common ground, nor are the virtues of compromise necessarily a part of the characteristic traits of the contestants.

Political arrangements superimposed by the great powers may, perhaps, resolve some of the immediate problems, but they do not appear as a satisfactory substitute for a durable solution via agreement mutually concurred in and arrived at; for the contesting states are hesitant, if not opposed to, any formula of settlement externally imposed. Yet, no settlement seems possible without the great powers participating in the agreement.

It is within this context that prior denunciation or noncompliance

[22] This is, of course, not to say that an armed conflict can exist only amongst recognized entities.

with the Security Council decision by Israel and Arab nations will have to be examined. As a matter of generalization, the United Nations is empowered to undertake certain punitive measures, such as suspension and expulsion, should a member state "persistently violate" the principles of the Charter. However, since these punitive measures (like all other measures of sanction) must be in "proportion" to the wrongs committed, and since the "wrong" committed in the specific context of the Middle East problem is not easy to define, proper treatment or evaluation of the noncomplying state or defying state is a difficult dilemma.

First, so long as the international community operates on a pretense of international law, which when closely examined lacks definite meaning, it would be a matter of practical impossibility to determine with any measure of accuracy the "wrongs" committed by a specific contestant. For instance, unless it is clearly established that Israeli actions (for that matter, those of Egypt) are not properly within the confines of the self-defense provision of Article 51, or that the Gulf of Aqaba is not a territorial sea, or that the concept of belligerency negates Israeli "innocent passage" through the Strait of Tiran, and the like, the practical necessity of defining "the wrong" in the specific context of the problem is beyond practicable reach.

Second, and as stated previously, the entire question of the Middle East problem has been handled by the Security Council under Chapter VI of the Charter, not under Chapter VII. The implicit objective of the chapter is not so much to find a "wrong-doer"; that is, a state guilty of "threat to the peace, breach of the peace, or act of aggression," but to find a peaceful mode of solution, given a dispute, preferably among the contestants and in conjunction with the Security Council recommendation. Implicitly, also, Chapter VI does not insist upon any one specific mode of solution, rather, the chapter encourages various means of peaceful settlement procedures. Again, the Security Council, either by design or accident, avoided the necessity of determining a "wrong-doer" in the contest.

Third, while defiance or noncompliance has been charged reciprocally by the contestants, it does not appear that any one party monopolized the "wrongs," although Israel appears to have violated more resolutions requiring specific actions.

Fourth, while defiance or noncompliance is a matter of grave concern, it is a difficult (if not impossible) task to determine precisely the extent or degree of "wrongs" involved which prompts the Council action.

Fifth, even if precise determination of the "wrong" were possible, it seems problematic as to what sanctions are to be utilized under the Charter. To the extent that the Charter speaks of punitive measures, it speaks of "suspension" of a "Member... against which preventive or enforcement action has been taken by the Security Council," but none of the contestants in the dispute has been a target of either "preventive" or "enforcement" action; and while the Charter speaks of expulsion when a "Member... has persistently violated the Principles of the Charter" (Article 6), such a step is possible only "by the General Assembly upon the recommendation of the Security Council," and, again, no such steps were taken nor are they likely to take place. Consider, for instance, the Council decision to examine the whole question under Chapter VI.

Finally, given the present status of international politics, and considering past performance of the United Nations in matters of this nature, it seems unlikely that the Organization will insist upon expulsion under Article 6 of the Charter, even if it is assumed that there in fact exists "persistent violation" of Charter principles. Presumably, the "functional necessity" of the United Nations at the present juncture of international relations tends to make it encourage conformity with the Charter principles by persuasion rather than by imposing punitive sanctions as a means of maintaining "peace".

This examination reveals that defiance to or noncompliance with UN resolutions is, in spite of its seriousness, left largely unheeded. Undeniably, a cumulative effect of the continued inattention or inability to answer to defiant practices would ultimately undermine the United Nations and its ideals. A warning may be appropriately made here that attention should be paid to both quantitative and qualitative aspects of defiant practices and adjustments should be sought. The answer in the form of preventive or corrective action rests not on the United Nations *per se* but on the judgment of world public opinion. It appears certain that in the case of long practice of one-sided defiance, world public opinion could turn against the state, yet such does not appear to be the case in the Middle East conflict.

CHAPTER IX

THE CASES OF INDONESIA, FRANCE, AND CUBA

INTRODUCTION

In this chapter, three cases of disassociation will be examined: Indonesian "withdrawal" from the United Nations; French refusal to participate in the North Atlantic Treaty Organization (NATO); and the Cuban "expulsion" from the Organization of American States (OAS). In spite of their physical disassociations from the respective international organizations, states concerned are or had to be regarded as members of the respective international organizations in law.

THE CASE OF INDONESIA

The Deputy Prime Minister and Minister of Foreign Affairs of Indonesia informed the Secretary-General of the United Nations, in a letter dated January 20, 1965, that his government had decided to withdraw from the United Nations effective March 1 of the same year (1) in protest to the seating of "neo-colonialist" Malaysia as a non-permanent member of the Security Council, and (2) because of circumstances "which have been created by colonial powers in the United Nations against the anti-colonial struggle and indeed against the lofty principles and purposes of the United Nations Charter." This decision set a precedent for which the Charter offered no guidance, and the issue became the center of discussion both within and without the United Nations.[1]

[1] Egon Schwelb, "Withdrawal From the United Nations: The Indonesian Intermezzo," *American Journal of International Law*, vol. 61 (1967), pp. 661-672; For the text of Indonesian letter, see *New York Times*, January 22, 1965.

In his letter of acknowledgment, the Secretary-General carefully avoided the word "withdrawal"; yet, for all practical purposes, Indonesia had disassociated itself from the United Nations as of the date specified in the original letter.[2]

Although Indonesia has been readmitted to, or has resumed its participation in, the United Nations, the issue of withdrawal in the absence of any Charter stipulation needs to be reexamined, and an answer, if possible, should be suggested. Such an inquiry must begin from the history and development of the United Nations in an effort to ascertain the intentions of the framers of the Charter regarding rights or privileges of withdrawal. Even here, problems exist.

Although the Charter is acknowledged to be silent on the subject, the conferences preceding its adoption addressed themselves to the problem. It must be added hastily that, while the intentions of the framers may be rationally deduced, it is doubtful that these unwritten understandings can be legally enforced, inasmuch as member states ratified the Charter with no explicit or implicit understandings (or reservations) other than the basic Charter stipulations. On the other hand, it would seem unreasonable to assert, at least initially, that sovereign states (and United Nations members supposedly are sovereign in the broad sense of that term) should be deprived of deviations from the Charter provision in its absolutes, including in this case absolute rejection of the privilege to disassociate themselves from the world organization, especially in absence of a specific provision in the Charter.[3] On this fine legal point, both scholars and practitioners of international law are devided.

The history of the United Nations reveals that the subcommittee of the Committee I/2 of the San Francisco Conference had felt that the Dumbarton Oaks Proposals intentionally omitted any mention of withdrawal rights in order to establish a permanent organization in which no member state could utilize the threat of withdrawal as a means of advancing claims or securing concessions from the organization. Hence, the committee decided to omit any mention of the rights of withdrawal, and instead inserted the following passage:[4]

[2] For further details, see Schwelb, *op. cit.*, p. 666.

[3] Hans Kelsen, *The Law of the United Nations,* (New York: Frederick A. Praeger, 1966), pp. 122-126.

[4] Schwelb, *op. cit.*, p. 663, see also Francis O. Wilcox and Carl M. Marcy, *Proposals for Changes in the United Nations,* (Washington: Brookings Institution, 1955), pp. 24-25.

The Committee adopts the view that the Charter should not make express provision either to permit or prohibit withdrawal from the Organization. The Committee deems that the highest duty of the nations which will become Members is to continue their co-operation within the Organization for the preservation of international peace and security. If, however, a Member because of exceptional circumstances feels constrained to withdraw, and leave the burden of maintaining international peace and security on the other Members, it is not the purpose of the Organization to compel that Member to continue its co-operation in the Organization.... It is obvious, particularly, that withdrawals or some other forms of dissolution of the Organization would become inevitable, if, deceiving the hopes of humanity, the Organization was revealed to be unable to maintain peace or could do so only at the expense of law and justice.... Nor would a Member be bound to remain in the Organization if its rights and obligations as such were changed by the Charter amendment in which it has not concurred and which it finds itself unable to accept, or if an amendment duly accepted by the necessary majority in the Assembly or in a general conference fail to secure the ratification necessary to bring such amendment into effect.... It is for these considerations that the Committee decided to abstain from recommending insertion in the Charter of a formal clause specifically forbidding or permitting withdrawal.

The foregoing indicates, in short, that an avenue for withdrawal seemed to be open for dissatisfied states although exercise of such rights was intentionally made available only on rare occasions. The report seems to find acceptable cause for the exercise of withdrawal rights when (1) "exceptional circumstances" exist, (2) a member's rights and duties are changed by the Charter amendment, or (3) the organization is revealed to be incapable of maintaining international peace and security, or does so at the expense of law and justice.[5]

It may be argued, as has been done, that the report makes withdrawal not only a possibility but provides conditions for disassociations by withdrawal. This supposition becomes less certain, however, when one asks when, how, and by whom these conditions will be determined.[6]

Inevitably, it would seem in a sense that each member nation is entitled to make that decision, for the Charter does not specify any organ or agency for that purpose. This line of argument seems to support the idea that a member nation may withdraw from the United Nations as a matter of right, even in absence of specific provisions on the issue.

On the other hand, it seems equally plausible to argue for the lack of withdrawal rights, for the Charter precludes any state, irrespective of its

[5] Kelsen, *op. cit.*, pp. 122-126.

[6] *Ibid.* See also Schwelb, *op. cit.*, pp. 661-672 and Wilcox and Marcy, *op. cit.*, p. 25.

membership status in the United Nations, from engaging in activities that directly or indirectly threaten international peace and security, presumably as determined by the United Nations; hence, complete disassociation from the United Nations seems an impossibility.[7]

In the specific case of Indonesia, a state has unilaterally decided to disassociate itself from the United Nations, Charter stipulations notwithstanding. From March of 1965 to September of 1966, it saw fit to remain outside the United Nations system and has refused to participate in United Nations forums.

A careful comparison of the alleged Indonesian reasons for withdrawal with the report of the Committee I/2 of the San Francisco Conference would reveal that one of the principal reasons for Indonesia's withdrawal—the election of nonpermanent members to the Security Council—cannot be regarded as a circumstance so "exceptional" in nature as to justify disassociation. It seems reasonably safe to observe that the inability of the United Nations to take definite action in this instance results more from the nature of contemporary bipolarized international politics than from inability to make a viable stand. Actions of the United Nations—rather, inaction or inability to take action—in this instance illustrate the extent of actual change that has taken place in the basic character of the organization, and are a clear signal for further changes. This pessimism, however, must not mask the potentiality, for deviations (or flexibility) from the static provisions of the often obsolete basic documents seem to be the very source of effectiveness in international organization.

When Indonesia decided to rejoin the organization, the issue was decided with noticeable calm and a minimum of legal or political difficulties; the president of the General Assembly merely requested that Indonesia's action be considered an absence or cessation of cooperation rather than a withdrawal, and that its full membership rights be restored upon meeting certain procedural (reflying the Indonesian flag, for instance) and administrative conditions (such as payment on the balance of assessment for the period of absence).[8]

If Indonesia had sought, through its "withdrawal", (1) to attain condemnation of the United Nations from the general community of states

[7] For a complete discussion on this point, see Leland M. Goodrich and Anne P. Simons, *The United Nations and the Maintenance of International Peace and Security*, 2nd printing, (Washington: Brookings Institution, 1957), pp. 128-141.

[8] Schwelb, *op. cit.*, pp. 661-672.

and (2) to perhaps unseat and discredit the Malaysian election to the Security Council as nonpermanent member, it cannot be said that Indonesia had succeeded in either of these goals. If, on the other hand, the goal of Indonesian "withdrawal" was to generally discredit and dishonor the United Nations, here too, Indonesia had failed; after all, Indonesia resumed association with the same organization under conditions set by the organization, including payment on the balance of assessment for the period of its absence.

Indonesia's resumption of cooperation with the United Nations marked the end of a chapter in the United Nations history on withdrawal; yet greater questions of future significance are still to be answered.

THE CASE OF FRANCE

The North Atlantic Treaty envisions an initial duration of validity for twenty years from the date of its promulgation. But within the first decade of the existence, indications of serious problems became apparent, the most significant of which, admittedly, at least for the purpose of this study, was the reduction of contributions by one of its principal signatories, France. As early as 1958, the French government began to reduce her share of naval units assigned to NATO, and the trend has persisted until now France is a "member in name" only.

It is not the purpose of this study to trace chronologically the developments leading to the present status. Suffice it to state that French "withdrawal" from NATO has been prompted by, among others, the following four reasons:[9]

1. "The center of international crisis" had moved from Europe to Asia "where the countries of the Atlantic Alliance as a group [were] obviously not involved," and, as a result, France was faced with an increased risk of being drawn into an unwanted war as long as it continued its participation in the American-dominated NATO structure.
2. The threat of an attack or subversion from the Soviet Union, which was the motivation for NATO, had subsided at least to the point of making the NATO military superstructure unnecessary, if not outright obstructive to reducing international tension.

[9] Eric Stein and Dominique Carreau, "Law and Peaceful Change in a Subsystem: 'Withdrawal' of France from the North Atlantic Treaty Organization," *American Journal of International Law*, vol. 62 (1968), p. 618.

3. Although nuclear weapons had emerged as the most important component of modern defense, the bulk of the Western nuclear arsenal remained "outside" NATO and this was one reason why France had to develop its own nuclear force of dissuasion.
4. The Soviet Union's acquisition of a massive nuclear arsenal had changed profoundly the world balance of power; the resulting direct threat to United States territory had reduced the credibility of the American commitment to employ its nuclear arsenal in case of an attack on Europe.

In terms of concrete actions, the French Government has:

1. "phased out" the French naval units assigned to NATO;
2. prohibited stockpiling of nuclear weapons on its territory;
3. prohibited over-flights of United States aircraft armed with nuclear weapons;
4. refused to participate in certain NATO maneuvers;
5. refused to accept NATO guidelines for the use of nuclear weapons in wartime;
6. failed to take its seat on the so-called "McNamara Committee" (composed of ten Defense Ministers of the 15 NATO nations) for nuclear planning;
7. terminated the assignment to NATO of its land and air forces stationed in Germany;
8. demanded the transfer of the two commands (Supreme Allied Command Europe and the Central Europe Command) out of the French territory;
9. made *de facto* separation from NATO principles.

These are a sample of some of the French actions based upon the considerations and reasons cited above. Yet, and significantly, the French government has never claimed *de jure* and complete disassociation from the Organization.[10]

Insofar as the basic stipulations of the treaty regarding withdrawal are concerned, Article 13 (which is the only article addressed to this eventuality) allows it only (1) after twenty years of initial existence and (2) "one year after [a member's] notice of denunciation." In short, the treaty does not foresee any possibility of disassociation (save possibly by route of *rebus sic stantibus*) until these two conditions have been met.

The suggestion has been made, at times, by such writers as Professors Eric Stein and Dominique Carreau [11] of the Michigan Law School, that although French disassociation from NATO cannot be based on any

[10] See *Ibid.*, and Carroll Quigley, "France and the United States in World Politics," *Current History*, vol. 54, no. 319 (1968), pp. 151-159, 180; Elliot R. Goodman, "De Gaulle's NATO Policy in Perspective," *ORBIS*, vol. 10, no. 3 (1966), pp. 690-723; John Davis Lodge, "Can NATO Be Restored," *ORBIS*, vol. 10, no. 3 (1966), pp. 724-736.

[11] For this and related points, see Stein and Carreau, *op. cit.*, pp. 577-640.

principle of law (save *rebus sic stantibus*), a military arrangement such as NATO cannot gain anything by enforcing membership; as Professors Stein and Carreau see it, "all parties concerned appeared to prefer [disassociation], as the lesser of two evils,.... evidently because they recognized the reality of the continuing common interests."

Yet, should prevalent politics within or without France turn in such a way that the French government should subsequently ask for "readmission," or "resumption of membership rights," one would be hardput to justify omission or negation of valid legal principles in favor of convenience and of immediate choice of "the lesser of two evils" at the present juncture.

In short, the French stand *vis-à-vis* NATO has many facets. At the very heart of the issue lay French refusal to be integrated into an "American system"—the system which subordinates, as France sees it, all interests to American will and strategy, both of which are questionable, obsolete, and inconsistent with French national interests.

In the French instance, as stated previously, there has never been, in a strict sense, a question of membership in NATO, for France has neither submitted a formal withdrawal notice nor has there been any juridical basis to negate French membership in the organization. It must be recalled that, as in the United Nations Charter, the North Atlantic Treaty provides no withdrawal stipulations, and while Article 13 of the treaty provides a possibility of termination of membership, such opportunity can only be utilized after twenty years of initial existence and "one year after [a member's] notice of denunciation." In short, the treaty does not foresee, prior to the time when the initial twenty years (1969) are up, any privilege of disassociation.

Hence, the French case too is a matter of non-participation rather than the question of membership, and, as in the Indonesion case, non-participation can at best be construed as "inactive" membership pending resumption of full participation—not as disassociation by "withdrawal."

In actual practice, however, it must be conceded that the French disassociation from NATO has had a far greater practical effect upon NATO than the Indonesian "withdrawal" from the United Nations. Afterall, NATO bases and its Headquarters had to be moved from French territory and, assuredly, French noncontribution to NATO forces and its nonparticipation in NATO activities (including military exercises) must have had a far greater impact upon NATO than the mere absence of Indonesia from the United Nations scene.

It appears reasonable to observe further that the real impact of disassociation, whatever juridical terms were used to describe the fact of disassociation, is dependent upon (1) not only on the completeness with which a member state terminates its relations with an international organization but also (2) on the physical influence ("power") of the disassociating state, and, finally, (3) on the extent to which the disassociating state's contribution in real terms (i.e., men and money) are essential to the overall accomplishment of the objectives of the organization concerned.

THE CASE OF CUBA

It is apparent from the foregoing cases that when the constitutive stipulation is put into actual practice, the lines between expulsion, suspension, and withdrawal are indeed fine and often indistinguishable. This point will become more apparent, possibly, by the examination of Cuban "expulsion" from the Organization of American States (OAS).

From the very outset, it must be recalled that at the Eighth Foreign Ministers Conference of OAS (Punta del Este, June, 1962), "the present Government" of Cuba was excluded from the Organization for its "adherence .... to the Marxist-Leninist ideology," which is deemed incompatible with the inter-American system.[12] Yet, in a strict legal sense, Cuba as a state is and has been a member of the OAS, although "the present Government" is deprived of its representation rights in OAS forums; the contrast with the previous two cases (Indonesia and France) being that in the case of Cuba *vis-à-vis* OAS, the initial move of disassociation came from the Organization, while in both the Indonesian and French instances, the states themselves initiated disassociation. In all cases, however, legal status of membership with the respective international organization remained unchanged.

It must be recalled that the OAS Charter has no stipulation regarding suspension or expulsion of a member nation. The question in the case of Cuba is, therefore, a determination of the validity of the OAS's exclusion of "the present Government" of Cuba in the absence of specific provision in the basic document.

[12] The Final Act of the Eighth Meeting of Consultation of Ministers of Foreign Affairs, January 31, 1962. The texts and related resolutions may be found in the *American Journal of International Law*, vol. 56 (1962), pp. 601-616.

It is alleged (1) that the present government of Cuba has violated certain obligations of OAS membership through its adherence to Marxism-Leninism including the obligations to reject "alliances or agreements that may lead to intervention in America by extra-continental powers," (2) that Cuba's connection with the Sino-Soviet bloc countries is incompatible with the principles and standards of the inter-American system and prevents her from fulfilling the obligations of the OAS Charter and the Rio Pact, (3) that Cuba's acceptance of military assistance from extra-continental powers allegedly breaks down the effectiveness of the inter-American system, and (4) that these grounds enable the OAS to exclude the present government of Cuba from the inter-American system.[13]

The legal question of OAS action *vis-à-vis* Cuba takes a lengthy detour. First of all it is argued that the OAS Charter (Article 25) invokes measures under the Rio Pact:

> [if] the inviolability or the integrity of the territory or the sovereignty or political independence of any American State should be affected by an armed attack or by an act of aggression that is not an armed attack, or by an extra-continental conflict... or by any other fact or situation that might endanger the peace of America.

It is further argued that the Rio Pact, in Article 6 for instance, provided the Organ of Consultation to agree on the "measures which should be taken for the common defense and for the maintenance of the peace and security of the Continent."

The second consideration involves examination of OAS action in view of Article 15 and 17 of the OAS Charter as compared with Article 19, and in view of Article 4 of the Rio Pact and Article 51 of the United Nations Charter. Article 15 of the OAS Charter obligates all members to noninterference "in the internal or external affairs of any other states," and Article 17 upholds the inviolability of the territories of member states. Article 19 emphatically states, however, that "measures adopted for the maintenance of peace and security.... do not constitute a violation of the principles set forth in Articles 15 and 17." Hence, if the decision to exclude the present government of Cuba was an action within the meaning of "measures adopted for the maintenance of peace and security," there seems to be no ground for appealing to Articles 15 and 17.

[13] See, for instance, Charles G. Fenwick, "Issues at Punta de Este: Non-Intervention versus Collective Security," *American Journal of International Law*, vol. 56 (1962), pp. 469-474.

In the final analysis, and whatever force might have been at play, by the fact that the exclusion decision was made with a two-thirds vote, it seems safe to assume that the Organization was satisfied that the decision fell within the meaning of Article 19 of the OAS Charter.[14]

Article 4 of the Rio Pact and Article 51 of the United Nations Charter state that measures of self-defense may be undertaken until the Security Council of the United Nations has taken the measures necessary to maintain international peace and security. But Article 53 of the United Nations Charter prohibits any "enforcement action under regional arrangements ... without the authorization of the Security Council." Hence, the question arises as to the definition of measures of "self-defense" and "enforcement action," and more particularly as to whether any of these Articles pertain to measures of nonmilitary self-defense such as the decision by a regional organization to cease formal relationships with a specific member nation.

The U.S. government justified the OAS action on the ground that the OAS has the right to interpret its own Charter and that such interpretation should be based on the principal purpose of the Charter; hence, should a regional organization—in this case, the OAS—decide that a member state has violated its obligations of the Charter, as has been so decided in the case of Cuba, it is completely within the right of the regional organization concerned to undertake appropriate measures.

This conclusion seems to be based on a highly restrictive interpretation of Article 53 but on a broad interpretation of Article 51 of the United Nations Charter and Article 4 of the Rio Pact.

In short, the U.S. government seems to be saying that Article 53, if applicable at all in this instance, is minimally valid, while Article 51 may be at issue; yet even the applicability of Article 51 was questioned on the ground that the OAS action against Cuba was merely a question of the right of a regional organization to determine its membership. In the final analysis, it is implicit that the Cuban issue is merely a case of collective renunciation by the OAS membership of the "present Government" of Cuba, as the similar right is implicitly vested in all international organizations, Article 53 of the Charter notwithstanding.

[14] For further discussion on this and related points, see Inis L. Claude, Jr., "The OAS, the UN and the United States," *International Conciliation,* No. 547 (1964), pp. 53-60; Robert N. Burr, *Our Troubled Hemisphere: Perspectives on United States-Latin American Relations,* (Washington: Brookings Institution, 1967), pp. 69-70.

OAS actions prior to the exclusion of the present government of Cuba serve to elaborate the point mentioned earlier that states may seek to avoid international obligations that may be imposed by the United Nations by pleading that the matter should be, or is being, settled by a regional organization. In fact, the OAS stands out as the regional organization in which there has been formal controversy on this point, and the debates regarding the exclusion of the present government of Cuba do not provide the only illustrations.[15]

When Cuba requested Security Council consideration of its charges of intervention against the United States, the latter responded immediately that the OAS was the proper forum. Cuba stressed its right to bring the charge directly to the Council. The United States rebutted by disclaiming designs against Cuba and pointing out that the OAS foreign ministers were meeting to deal with the matter. The basis for the final resolution was hazy, but the Council appears to have referred the case to the OAS without formally deciding that the regional organization had priority in jurisdiction. Cuba next appealed to the General Assembly and, while the Assembly's First Committee considered the matter, to the Security Council a second time. The Council took no action. When the first Committee began its consideration at a later date, the Bay of Pigs invasion had occurred and the United States had admitted its involvement. The resolution that was finally passed contained very little to suggest that the OAS should have priority in handling the matter; it called upon all members to promote peaceful settlement without recognizing a special role for the regional organization.

When OAS suspended Cuba in 1962, it also suspended the usefulness of the argument that Cuba should apply to the regional organization before appealing to the United Nations.[16]

[15] When Guatemala bypassed the OAS and asked the Security Council to consider its charge of aggression by Nicaragua and Honduras in 1954, the Soviet Union vetoed a resolution that would have referred the matter to OAS. Although the Council voted to call for termination of the invasion and to request states to refrain from assisting the attackers, it failed to adopt the agenda the second time Guatemala urged it to consider the question. As a consequence Guatemala agreed to cooperate with the OAS, but before the regional organization acted, a new government took over in Guatemala and informed the Council that the case was closed. For details of this case and the Dominican, Haitian and Panamanian cases, see Claude, *op. cit.*, pp. 21-34, 43-46, 48-53.

[16] *Ibid.*, pp. 34-43, 53-60.

SUMMARY

An international organization is:[17]

> a collectivity of States established by treaty, with a constitution and common organs, having a personality distinct from that of its Member-States, and being a subject of international law with treaty-making capacity.

What is implicit in this definition is that, while each state is free and independent to decide whether it will join a particular international organization, a similar freedom and independence is not to be assumed once a state joins an international organization for henceforth the treaty itself becomes a delimiting force in the exercise of that state's freedom of action.

In the cases of Indonesia and France, the former withdrew under a Charter that is silent on the matter, while French disassociation (amounting to nonparticipation) from NATO activities took place during the initial twenty-year period during which time the treaty implicitly demands unaltered cooperation by all members.

Discussions on the consistency of the two incidents with general principles of international law seem to center around two schools of thought: on the one hand, some hold that, since international organization is a product of a multilateral treaty, the points of crucial legal import are those legal norms which govern treaties; on the other, some seem to hold that the legality of disassociation is to be judged solely on the basis of intent (explicitly stated or implicitly inferred) of the framers of the organization.[18]

Undoubtedly, problems exist when under one view certain rights are entertained while under the other the same rights are denied, as is seemingly the case here.

The former view seems to be based on the concepts of *rebus sic stantibus* and the concept of "sovereignty"; the latter view centers on the general practice of international organization, which includes disassociation of members normally under (a) dissolution of the international organization, (b) voluntary withdrawal under the terms of respective basic documents, (c) suspension, and (d) expulsion.

[17] I.L.C. *Yearbook*, (1956), vol. 2, p. 108.

[18] For this and related points, see N. Feinberg, "Unilateral Withdrawal from An International Organization," *British Yearbook of International Law*, vol. 39 (1963), pp. 189-219.

Upon closer examination, relying on the concept of *rebus sic stantibus* seems to lose its otherwise due weight when it is considered that neither the Indonesian nor the French government specifically relied on *rebus sic stantibus*. Furthermore, to argue in favor of the existence of withdrawal rights based on the concept of *rebus sic stantibus* would be to acknowledge absence of the right under the respective constitutive acts.[19]

The thesis that there exists right of withdrawal on the basis of the concept of "sovereignty" is likewise questionable for it is seemingly based on the premise that since an international organization is a loose confederal machinery ordained by member nations which retain their soveignties, each member nation is free to determine whether it wishes to continue, or discontinue, its association with that organization. But this analogy needs support in law. In addition, it ignores the particulars of each case, for at minimum, it does not seem plausible to state that this general theory of confederation is necessarily applicable in all international institutions, and, there is not sufficient agreement among the writers on this point to justify the claim.[20]

Additionally, the experiences under the League of Nations as well as under the United Nations seem to indicate that omission of the right of withdrawal in basic documents seems to have been taken as negating the existence of such a right. The framers of the Covenant of the League seem to have assumed that the right of withdrawal is absent unless expressly provided; hence, the Covenant provides two avenues of withdrawal in its basic document.[21]

[19] *Ibid.*

[20] For a discussion on the applicability of *rebus sic stantibus* concept, see William L. Tung, *International Law in an Organizing World,* (New York: Thomas Y. Crowell Co., 1968), pp. 356-359. Professor Fenwick states, in this connection, that: "This rule [rebus sic stantibus] is logically deducible from the general principle that a state cannot be presumed to have bargained away the very conditions of its continued existence as an international person unless it has done so in clear and explicit terms." See Charles G. Fenwick, *International Law,* 4th ed., (New York: Appleton-Century-Crofts, 1965), pp. 545-546. For a discussion on the rationales behind the concept of "sovereignty" and the theory of confederation as a basis for the existence of right of withdrawal, see N. Feinberg, *op. cit.,* pp. 212-214. For a brief discussion on the issue of dissociation from international organizations, see Elmer Plischke, *International Relations,: Basic Documents,* 2nd ed., (Princeton, N.J.: D. Van Nostrand Co., 1962), p. 51.

[21] For one, the Covenant of the League provides in Article 1 (3) that: "Any Member of the League may, after two years' notice of its intention to do so, withdraw from the League, provided that all its international obligations and all its

Furthermore, the practices of international organizations seem to dictate that, in the absence of any specific stipulation on withdrawal in the basic documents, unilateral withdrawal is commonly regarded as a voluntary decision not to exercise participation rights rather than termination of formal membership with an organization.

Thus Argentina did not take part in the works of the League for twelve consecutive years prior to 1933, and Bolivia and Peru abstained from participation in the League for seven years prior to 1929. In all these cases, the League regarded the states' return not as cases of readmission but as "resumption" of participation.[22] Similarly, the World Health Organization and the United Nations Educational, Scientific, and Cultural Organization regarded similar experiences as, again, "resumption" of participation.

In a related context (and notwithstanding the original intentions of the framers of the North Atlantic Treaty for the continued existence during the first twenty years), the French government's refusal to participate can be regarded only as nonparticipation wholly unrelated to French membership in the organization.

It appears, therefore, to be a reasonable generalization that unless the basic document stipulates, explicitly or implicitly, the presence of and prescription for the right of withdrawal, a state is not at liberty to disassociate from an international organization: the silence of the basic document is no basis for the assumption of withdrawal rights. Additionally, while a state is not at liberty to withdraw in the absence of specific constitutive provisions, nonparticipation, while it may amount to actual withdrawal, is well within the prerogative of the member states.

The records of international organizations seem to suggest that an examination of the legal validity of withdrawal should consider whether (1) a withdrawal clause exists in the basic document, (2) withdrawal is complete or partial, and (3) withdrawal is voluntary or involuntary.

First, where the basic documents provide specific stipulations for withdrawal, as in the instances of FAO, WMO, ILO, or the League of Nations,

obligations under this Covenant shall have been fulfilled at the time of its withdrawal."

Additionally, in Article 26 (2), the Covenant states: "No ... amendment shall bind any Member of the League which signifies its dissent therefrom, but in that case it shall cease to be Member of the League," Hence, the privilege of dissociation under Article 26, par. 2 amounts to an automatic withdrawal.

[22] Feinberg, *op. cit.*, p. 192.

and where a member state withdraws in accordance with respective provisions, rights of withdrawal seem unquestionable both in law and practice. However, as the Indonesian case seems to illustrate, absence of specific withdrawal provisions in the basic document does create some difficulty; at minimum, it seems safe to state that an absence should not be regarded *ipso facto* permission or prevention *per se* for withdrawal.

In the final analysis, should the case be made for withdrawal in absence of a specific provision in the basic document, it will have to be based, among other criteria, on the definition and implication of the concept of absolute "sovereignty," or, perhaps, on the doctrine of *rebus sic stantibus*, wherein a member nation is taken as the final arbiter of the changed circumstances and possesses unlimited and unchallengeable rights. Yet, this unlimited and broad definition of "sovereignty" and unilateral determination of the *rebus sic stantibus* doctrine obviously cannot enjoy the blessing of the contemporary international community.

Second, while the term "partial withdrawal" is not used in many constitutive documents (at least among those of which the writer is aware), some international organizations do engage in a practice that is in fact no more than a "partial withdrawal." For instance, when the issues of South Africa's withdrawal from the International Labor Organization (1961-64) had been debated, the Director-General was of the opinion that South Africa could be excluded from all forums sponsored by the Governing Board, but that her participation in the International Labor Conference could not be questioned since this forum was created by a direct mandate of the ILO constitution, which is silent on expulsion. In this case, it seems clear that the forced withdrawal of South Africa from ILO was in fact partial, at least until 1964 when it actually and completely disassociated itself from the organization.

A complete withdrawal, on the other hand, is an actual and total disassociation from an international organization and presumably from its sub-systems and dependent organizations as well. But contemporary international relations create problems here also. For instance, while some specialized organizations of the United Nations, such as UNESCO and IMCO, have very close if not indistinguishable ties with the United Nations on the problem of expulsion, others such as IMF, IBRD, and IFC maintain independent policies on the same issue. Hence, expulsion of a member from the United Nations may effect automatic disassociation of the same members from some but not from all the specialized organizations.

Third, determining whether withdrawal is voluntary or involuntary is not as easy as it may appear to be. For all practical purposes, for instance, South Africa's "withdrawal" from ILO was forced upon that nation by the organization, although technically it may be termed a withdrawal. Additionally, diplomatic niceties, flowery language, unofficial premaneuverings, and the like often make determination of the original initiative very difficult. The basic test seems theoretically to be dependent upon ascertaining the original initiative; the problem, in short, is to decide at what point in time the test of initiative comes in.

The crucial point appears to be that the absence of a specific provision respecting withdrawal was taken, in the Indonesian and French cases, as delimiting the prerogative of the organization, while, in the Cuban incident, the reverse was true—that is, absence of the specific provision (namely, expulsion) was taken as a legal grant of power to the organization. Additionally, judging from the OAS action against Cuba, an international organization may even go so far as to include a state (and people thereof) as a member, yet exclude the specific government as its spokesman.

In the same vein, it seems reasonably safe to observe that the inability of the United Nations to take definite action on the Indonesian incident results more from the nature of contemporary bipolarized international politics than from inability to make a viable stand. Actions of the United Nations (rather, inaction or inability of action) in this instance illustrate the extent of actual change that has taken place in the basic character of the organization, and are a clear signal for further changes.

In the final analysis, it appears that the specificity of the language, or the existence or lack of particular provisions in the basic documents, seems to matter less than the collective will of the member states. This is true even if the collective will is inconsistent with the basic document. In short, inaction by the organization, or even a counteraction, sometimes has to be regarded as the intended will of the organization. Yet, again, this response is not to be taken as a sign of weakness; for the essence of most international organizations in the final analysis is their confederal nature (of various degrees) and, therefore, their dependence upon member states for power, functions, and even survival.

By the same token, resort to disassociation, whether initiated by states against international organizations or *vise versa*, does not, it appears, succeed in securing concessions from the other party. While OAS, for instance, sought to expel Cuba from the Inter-American system thereby presumably to discourage its continued adherence to the Marxist-Leninist doctrine and sought further to isolate it from the hemispheric nations, the record thus far reveals that Cuba has been far from isolated from the hemispheric nations or from the world community in general.

Indonesia has sought to defy the United Nations and thereby presumably to signify to the world its ability to be independent without its association to the United Nations, and, too, to condemn the "colonial powers in the United Nations [which are] against the anticolonial struggle." It, too, has presumably argued against its own allegation and decided to return to the United Nations without the latter making any concessions to Indonesia.

French disassociation from NATO, likewise, failed to bring about any significant concession from the organization ; in spite of French rejection of the validity of NATO principles, NATO is still a viable reality.

In the final analysis, disassociations from international organizations initiated by states, it appears, neither free the states from international obligations nor coerce the international organizations concerned to substantially alter their basic edicts; in the same manner, international organizations too appear unable to coerce states to accept obligations against their will by expulsion or suspension.

CHAPTER X

THE CASE OF THE PEOPLE'S REPUBLIC OF CHINA (PRC)

INTRODUCTION

Consideration of PRC's participation, or lack of it, in the United Nations and its defiance of the United Nations in Korea must include a brief survey of the particulars of the circumstances within and without China that are collectively responsible for its relations with the United Nations. Hence, the present discussion will include: (1) a brief historical survey of PRC with emphasis on its external policies; (2) a review of PRC's experience with the United Nations; (3) an evaluation of performance; and (4) an examination of PRC's defiance.

SURVEY OF PRC GOVERNMENT

The People's Republic of China became a reality as a consequence of the many, and at times untraceable, turns of events within China, which occurred not totally without outside influence and assistance. A combination of circumstances, ineffectiveness and overburdens assumed by the Chiang government, the lack of an informed populace and dependable economic and political bases, pressures from without (especially from Japan), excessive optimism on the part of the United States, the anxiety of the Soviet Union for an Asian ally, among others, moved events to the latter half of the 1940's when, in October 1949, the regime headed by a professional revolutionary, Mao Tse-tung, was formally established as the People's Democratic Republic of China.

By that time, the *Kuo Min Tang* (KMT) government, headed by Chiang Kai-shek, had been deprived of its foothold in mainland China and exiled in Taiwan—the santuary founded by American military protection.

It seems sufficient to state that the success of the revolutionary regime in the mainland is attributable to at least three main considerations: (1) growing discontent among the masses of China (mainly peasants, of course) over their increasingly degrading and degenerating lives—a trend which can be traced back beyond the founding of the Communist Party of China (CPC) in 1921 to the period of revolutionary fervor of 1910; (2) inability or unwillingness, or both, of the KMT government to cure the domestic ills and uplift the national life; (3) existence of an avenue of opposition to the KMT Government in the form of the CPC (Communist Party of China) which capitalized on the discontentment and internal discipline within the party to challenge effectively the established authority.

In this sense, the success of the CPC marked a culmination of revolutionary fervor within China which dates back to the first decade of the twentieth century. Chiang himself is a part of this fervor, except that his mandate came at the time when the external challenge to China was the greatest and most immediate, and the turn of events (again, both within and without China) did not give him the necessary "breathing spell" to consolidate sufficiently his position and power. The CPC's success was, on the other hand, marked by the end of "the war of all wars," wherein the principal powers were resolved to find paths of inter-state relationships without the recourse to wars. In fact, the sentiment of the mid-1940's was one of anti-war "at all cost," and the characteristic words of the time were "peace" and "cooperation," not "war" and "intervention."

Blessed by worldwide optimism for a "new order," and by intensified and a still very real revolutionary zeal within for "a new China" (a union more dignified, independent, and capable of being received as a co-equal in the international community), the Mao regime was able to capitalize on the Chinese "lot" of that time for its benefit and eventual success.

Whatever may be the theoretical or ideological justification, the CPC's success cannot, it appears, be separated from the foregoing considerations.

Having thus entered into the world community with what may be termed a sense of "mission" and "crusade," the PRC regime unhesitatingly clothed itself with many colors and images. Seemingly caring very little about attitudes of the non-Chinese world, it demanded what it thought was properly Chinese (if need be by threats and military actions) and subscribed to (or defied) norms of international intercourse only when it felt such was in the Chinese interest. Hence, from the time of its participation in support of North Korea during the Korean conflict, PRC has been unbending in employing any means at its disposal to advance whatever vision its leaders may care to entertain regarding the status of the East-West contest, "wars of national liberation," and the role (real or imagined) of PRC. The use of militancy in pursuance of what it regards as being rightly Chinese knows neither the conditions of contemporary international norms, nor the real capability of Chinese reach.[1] These are the forces which mark the PRC's image of, and lack of participation in, the United Nations, until the recent change in 1971.

PRC'S EXPERIENCE WITH THE UNITED NATIONS[2]

PRC's condemnation of the United Nations as a "tool of imperialism," which once marked the Chinese attitude toward the United Nations, is in sharp contrast to its initial warm reception of the Organization's basic principles and to its recent decision to associate with the United Nations.

Although it is always difficult to generalize the performance of the Chinese regime vis-a-vis the United Nations, its record tends to reveal certain relatively well-defined phases. The initial Chinese attitude toward the United Nations was, it appears, one of cordiality and concurrence with the ideals of the United Nations, prompted perhaps in part by undeniable gratitude to the Western Powers (including the Soviet Union) for their defeat of China's historic antagonist, Japan. It appears that this attitude prevailed at least until the outbreak of the Korean war. Cemented by the newly formalized alliance with the Soviet Union, and still crudely organized as a government within, the regime appeared to have viewed the United Nations as one more instrument through which its ambition for global recognition might be satisfied; accordingly, the regime insisted upon its rightful place in the United Nations, and demanded that the representatives of the Republic of China (ROC) be expelled from the United Nations. This initial response to the United Nations was matched by a relatively violent change in the succeeding few years.

Either because its security was thought to be threatened by the events surrounding the Korean war, or because of its self-confidence as *the* "new

[1] For further detail and analysis of Communist China's record of foreign relations, see A. Doak Barnett, "The United States and Communist China," *The United States and the Far East,* 2nd ed., Willard L. Thorp, ed., (New York: Prentice-Hall, Inc., 1962), pp. 98-157.

[2] See, for instance, Mostafa Rajai, "Communist China and the United Nations," *ORBIS,* vol. 10, no. 3 (Fall, 1966), pp. 823-838.

China," the regime became extraordinarily arrogant and the tone of its external policies characteristically became uncompromising. It is during this period that the regime intervened in Korea and gave open support to the "wars of national liberation" in Indo-China, Burma, Indonesia, and the like. In so doing it abandoned for a time one of its two demands of the United Nations; namely, it presumably decided to reject the United Nations as an instrument of global recognition. It retained the second demand, the ouster of "the Chiang Kai-shek gang".

Claiming that the United Nations is "a tool of imperialism" (initially of American imperialism but later that of the Soviet Union, as well), the regime defied the opportunity provided it by the United Nations in November 1950 in connection with discussion on the Korean war. General Wu Hsiu-ch'uan, speaking on behalf of the Chinese (PRC) delegation, and having arrived in New York at the invitation of the United Nations, categorically denied the validity of United Nations action in Korea, termed it "illegal," and demanded instead sanctions against the United States for its actions in Korea. This event was followed by what appears to be a counter-measure *in kind*; on February 1, 1951, the General Assembly of the United Nations passed a resolution condemning the Peiping government as an "aggressor" and, in May, followed with a recommendation for an embargo to PRC and North Korea. In its turn, the PRC attitude toward the United Nations became increasingly hostile and daring, focusing upon its "rightful" place in the United Nations of which it has been allegedly deprived principally by the efforts of the United States.

The language of the resolutions condemning PRC as an "aggressor" follows:[3]

The General Assembly...

Noting that the Security Council, because of lack of unanimity of the permanent members, has failed to exercise its primary responsibility for the maintenance of international peace and security in regard to Chinese Communist intervention in Korea,

Noting that the Central People's Government of the People's Republic of China has not accepted United Nations proposals to bring about a cessation of hostilities in Korea with a view to peaceful settlement, and that its armed forces continue their invasion of Korea and their large-scale attacks upon United Nations forces there,

1. Finds that the Central People's Government of the People's Republic of China, by giving direct aid and assistance to those who were already committing

[3] G.A.O.R., Fifth Session, Supplement No. 20A (A/1775/Add. 1), p. 1.

aggression in Korea and by engaging in hostilities against United Nations forces there, has itself engaged in aggression in Korea;

2. Calls upon the Central People's Government of the People's Republic of China to cause its forces and nationals in Korea to cease hostilities against the United Nations forces and to withdraw from Korea;

The economic and arms embargo against China states:[4]

The General Assembly...

1. Recommends that every state:
   (a) Apply an embargo on the shipment to areas under the control of the Central People's Government of the People's Republic of China and of the North Korea authorities of arms, ammunition and implements of war, atomic energy materials, petroleum, transportation materials of strategic value, and items useful in the production of arms, ammunition and implements of war.

To PRC, these were further material proof that the Organization was a forum for conspiracy among the United States-led, anti-Chinese groups to reduce mainland China in the international community and to deprive it of the seat which it rightly deserved. So long as the Korean conflict continued, PRC defiance of United Nations actions in Korea, and the demand for its seat in the Security Council continued unaltered. But this position has changed in the succeeding few years.

From about 1954 to the latter part of the 1950's (1956/7), the regime gave the appearance of comparatively restrained arrogance and resolved its seemingly hopeless plea for a seat in the United Nations. The regime seemed temporarily resolved to leave the United Nations issue at a standstill while pursuing the policy of "Afro-Asian Solidarity." It was during this period (1955) that the Bandung Conference of Asian-African Nations was held and PRC reportedly showed its magnificence and mastery of contemporary diplomacy (to the amazement of Western nations); a year earlier (1954), China had "triumphed" in Geneva over the resolution of the Indo-Chinese war. It was also during this period that the regime's "peace diplomacy" found expressions in the forum of *Five Principles of Peaceful Co-existence.*

It is reasonable to assume that the regime might have had expectations of a "new" United Nations, represented by the majority of Afro-Asian nations whose policies would differ substantially from the original and principally Western nations, a presumably favorable circumstance for the PRC. Such a reconstituted body would recognize that, "for the United

[4] *Ibid.*, p. 2.

Nations to carry out truly and effectively its duty of safeguarding world peace and international security, it would be essential, first of all, to restore to the People's Republic of China its legitimate rights in the United Nations."

After the historic Soviet feat in Sputnik in 1957, the PRC appeared to be convinced that "the East Wind" would indeed prevail over the West. Unhesitatingly, it undertook a harsh economic embargo against Japan, threatened Indonesia for its treatment of the Chinese in that country, took part (though indirectly) in the war in Laos, and fought military skirmishes on the Sino-Indian border. Its arrogance was again answered in the United Nations, though indirectly, in the form of a significant change in the voting procedure for the Chinese representation question. The new resolution, sponsored by New Zealand and obviously supported by the United States, made the question of Chinese representation a "substantive" matter, hence one requiring a two-thirds majority for approval. This almost impossible requirement infuriated the PRC, so much so that the regime seemingly abandoned the traditional plea for a seat in the organization and subsequently sought to establish a "United Nations" of its own. Hence, in hindsight, the first years of the 1960's marked a culminating point, during which time the PRC seemingly made an "about face" to the whole notion of the United Nations.

After 1962/3, the regime demanded certain concessions or a retreat in the United Nations' past activities as a price for its participation in the Organization. As for its early plea for a seat in the United Nations, the regime seemed perfectly content to dare the organization to maintain "international peace" without the cooperation of China; in fact, the PRC exhibited doubts as to the merits of joining the Organization, even if all its demands were met.

If PRC had made an about face to the United Nations, the same cannot be said of the various advocates of Chinese admission to the United Nations.[5] Initially headed by the Soviet Union, spokesmen for a Chinese

[5] In this connection, see, for instance, Myres S. McDougal and Richard M. Goodman, "Chinese Participation in the United Nations," *American Journal of International Law,* vol. 60 (1966), pp. 671-727; Nagendra Singh, *Termination of Membership of International Organizations,* (New York: Frederick A. Praeger, Inc., 1958), pp. 154-181; Hungdah Chiu, "Communist China's Attitude Toward the United Nations: A Legal Analysis," *American Journal of International Law,* vol. 62, (1968), pp. 20-50; Stephen S. Goodspeed, *The Nature and Function of International Organization,* 2nd ed., (New York: Oxford University Press, 1967), pp. 140-143; "Handbook on Communist China," *INTERCOM,* vol. 10, no. 5 (1968).

seat in the United Nations have slowly but surely increased in number. And whether this increase was due to sincere belief in the justice in the Chinese seat (however reasoned), or due perhaps to considerations related to the basic changes in the membership of the United Nations (both in quantity and quality), or due to the real or imagined trust in the inevitability of US-USSR *detente*, or whatever, the problem of a Chinese seat in the United Nations became an annual ritual, though without significant result, until the 1971 decision to seat PRC representatives.

Whatever may be said regarding the demands of PRC and the communist bloc on the admissions question, those states which have supported the admission of PRC have relied on one or more of the following arguments justifying the admission of PRC to the United Nations:

1. That PRC is the legitimate government of all China;
2. That the manner in which PRC came into power in China (i.e., through revolution) is essentially a matter of domestic jurisdiction, hence immune from international interference including that of the United Nations;
3. That the United Nations would merely be a name, or term, having no real meaning, if it excludes PRC which controls 800 million Chinese and a vast majority of Chinese territory, a nation which is becoming a major global power;
4. That the United Nations cannot hope to maintain international peace and security without the support and cooperation of PRC;
5. That PRC has been recognized by a significant number of states, a mark of its legitimate status as a member of international community.

On the other hand, opposition to admission of PRC has been based on one or more of the following considerations:

1. That PRC came into power by illegal means (by use of force) and that the United Nations' admission of PRC would directly or indirectly signify admissibility and encouragement of political change through the use of force (or other violent means);
2. That ROC is the government which signed the Charter of the United Nations in 1945 and has been the Government representing China ever since;
3. That ROC has committed no acts which constitute violations of the Charter and which could justify termination of its membership, even though its sphere of actual control in China has been reduced by the insurgent political group (PRC);
4. That PRC is the very regime which defied all norms of "national behavior" expressed in the United Nations Charter and, in fact, waged a war against the United Nations, and was condemned as an "aggressor" by the organization, an accusation most serious under the Charter;
5. That the general standards of behavior of PRC reveal that the regime is anything but "peace loving," and that it is "unable" and "unwilling" to carry out the obligations of the Charter;

6. That is it neither a "state" under the norms of international law, since it has come into power in violation of them, nor does it accept the obligations of the Charter, having defied and continuing to defy the United Nations by terming it as an "instrument of exploitation" and "legitimization" used by the capitalists to promote their interests;
7. That the advocates of PRC's admission assume that PRC, if admitted, would display positive, cooperative attitudes, a position which opponents of PRC's admission say appear indeed tenuous when considering PRC's past behavior. And that it would be a disservice to mankind if PRC were admitted, because the effect might be to hamper rather than to strengthen the United Nations.

Although the foregoing arguments have been much used, the main contests between advocates and opponents of the Chinese question have relied on various procedures which are often confusing.

The proponents of PRC representation, at least since 1961, centered their strategy on the thesis which, stated in brief, says that China is and has been a member of the United Nations, but denies the right of ROC to represent the Chinese people and China. Naturally, the proponents of PRC's admission claimed that since PRC controls almost all of the Chinese people and territory, PRC should be accorded the privilege of representing China.

However, the above claims are countered specifically by two resolutions which have been adopted by the General Assembly. The two resolutions reveal that the intent of the framers of the Charter was to limit the membership of the United Nations to certain states which meet certain predetermined qualifications, as judged by the collective membership, and that the United Nations was never meant to be an organization whose membership extends to any and all applicant states irrespective of their legal status, conduct or behavior in the international community. General Assembly resolution 396(V) requires that the "representation" decision be made "in the light of the Purposes and Principles of the Charter and the circumstances of each case," and Resolution 1668(XI) specifically labels the Chinese question as "important" for voting purposes, thus requiring two-thirds majority.

Therefore, the principal battle between proponents and opponents of PRC's representation has been waged in the political arena over the efforts to secure the necessary two-thirds majority required under the resolution above-cited.

In the twenty-year history of the Chinese issue (1950-1970), 19 actual votes were taken (there was no voting in 1964 due to financial problems). The pro-PRC bloc at all times received less than a simple majority, except in 1970. It was during the 1970 session of the General Assembly that the proponents of PRC's admission first received a simple majority (actual votes were: 51 in favor, 49 in opposition, and 25 in abstentention, out of 127 member states). Blessed by the sudden turnabout in the United States attitude and apparent repercussions of the same to other member states, the unprecedented voting majority has decided, in 1971, to favor PRC over the ROC as representative of China (actual votes were 76 in favor to 35 against with 17 abstentions).

EVALUATION OF PERFORMANCE

Upon reflection, acceptance of the norms of international obligations does not always serve or strengthen nations or their national interests, at least at this juncture of international relations; in fact, it must be admitted that as long as international politics and power considerations dictate the rights and wrongs of a state, and while the determination of what is right and therefore legal under international law is arrived at through political means (based on political motives for political ends), and as long as the international community is either unwilling or unable to make a clear distinction between the realms of law and of politics, it is understandable that the standard of judgment for an individual state will significantly vary according to prestige and influence of the concerned party.

In the specific case of China, therefore, if it be that politics and political considerations were to dictate the Chinese issue, the groundwork for its eventual admission was laid, as one looks back, in the fundamental change in American external policy best characterized by the so-called Nixon Doctrine, and the equally significant pronouncement of Nixon's visit to Peiping; the former was a warning for pro-Western and American allies to be independent from the accustomed "American nursery", and the latter was a clear and explicit signal that the Washington government was to indeed make an about face to its traditional China policy.

Prompted partly by the changed American posture on the China issue, and frenzied by the possibility of success in their struggle for securing a seat for China, and encouraged by the voting majority of 1970, the advocates for Chinese membership had renewed their pleas for a Chinese seat in 1971, having assurance of American silence, if not an all out support. The outcome was predictable; the Albanian resolution [Albania and twenty two other countries sponsored resolution 2758(XXVI)] states:

"The General Assembly,
"Recalling the principles of the Charter of the United Nations,
"Considering that the restoration of the lawful rights of the People's Republic of China is essential both for the protection of the Charter of the United Nations and for cause that the United Nations must serve under the Charter,
"Recognizing that the representatives of the Government of the People's Republic of China are the only lawful representatives of China to the United Nations and that People's Republic of China is one of the five permanent members of the Security Council,
"Decides to restore all its rights to the People's Republic of China and to recognize the representatives of its Government as the only legitimate representatives of China to the United Nations, and to expel forthwith the representatives of Chiang Kai-shek from the place which they unlawfully occupy at the United Nations and in all the organizations related to it."

Implicit in the resolution was:

1. That the problem of Taiwan and PRC is to be regarded as a Chinese domestic problem;
2. That the decision reveals that the limitations on legal or formal prescription of the Charter are subject to the then prevalent international politics;
3. That the United Nations itself indirectly, through its verdict on the Republic of China, encouraged each nation to rely on its own means for survival, including avoidance noncompliance, or defiance to the United Nations' norms;
4. That the power politics still precedes international agreements, at least in the crucial questions involving vital national interests;
5. That the United States has lost its previous majority on many of the key issues;
6. That the United Nations itself follows rather than leads the tone and climate of international politics, so much so that it may even contradict its own previous decisions or verdicts or at minimum remain untroubled by its contradicting actions.

From the recent United Nations decision on China, it appears reasonable to inquire about the status and implicit assumptions of defiant activity. Presumably, a given activity is defiant, provided that (1) the prevalent international politics does not significantly alter the standard to which the defiant state objects, and (2) that subsequent actions of the organization do not, either explicitly or implicitly, change the defiant status of a state, and (3) that the decision-making majority remains reasonably unchanged. After all, how else could the Albanian resolution be interpreted, in view of all the previous condemnation of PRC by the United Nations?

Likewise, the PRC's entry into the United Nations reveals that its previous pronouncement as to its conditions for association with the United Nations are more matters of traditional diplomatic maneuvers than of fundamental policy statements; it is recalled that PRC has implicitly abandoned all conditions for its membership in the United Nations other than the expulsion of ROC (i.e., revocation of resolution labeling it as an "aggressor" in the Korean war, and adoption of resolution condemning the United States as the "aggressor" in the Korean conflict, and the like, were seemingly abandoned by PRC).

Although PRC's entry into the United Nations tends to implicitly negate or at minimum makes various former United Nations resolutions vis-a-vis PRC *de facto* meaningless, a few points of considerable import might be observed.

First, there is presumably no limitations on the powers and functions of the United Nations on any matter over which there is a significant and necessary voting majority; implicitly, the recent decision to recognize the representatives of PRC as the *only legitimate representatives* of the government and people of China signifies the extent to which the United Nations can make decisions regarding legitimacy of a government.

Second, if the paramount consideration for the PRC's admission to the United Nations was due to considerations of its "power," (and conversely, ROC's expulsion was due to its lack of "power"), then should it not be that the same test of "power" be applied to, say, British and French membership in the Security Council? Should not one or both be replaced as well for reasons of "power"? In fact, what will prevent a decision-making majority in the General Assembly from expelling any other permanent members of the Security Council? What would indeed be the real merit of the United Nations if and when that occurs?

Third, if pragmatic power and power politics were indeed to dictate the membership question, the very existence of the United Nations can be questioned; for one of the very important goals of the United Nations was, it seems, to be beyond the immediate dictates of power politics. And could it not be alleged that the recent action by the United Nations on Chinese question may be interpreted as an encouragement for any insurgent groups to challenge the established authority so long as there is a reasonable assurance of success and/or so long as there is a voting majority in the United Nations to judge its legitimacy.

AN EXAMINATION OF PRC'S DEFIANCE

Depending upon one's selection of specific period, extent and intensity of PRC's defiance vis-a-vis United Nations will vary considerably. Upon reflection, the very heart of PRC's defiance centers around the events surrounding the Korean war—specifically, over the question of its participation in the war in defiance of United Nations enforcement action—and subsequent developments in Asia.

Additionally, claims and counter-claims over the PRC's role in Korea has had varied implications and justification. Within the narrow confines of the norms of the Charter and general principles of international law, the issue of defiance centers around: (1) the PRC's claim of self-defense and related supporting arguments in justification of its action in Korea *versus* the validity of United Nations enforcement action undertaken in accordance with Chapter VII of the Charter; (2) the PRC's claim of immunity from the United Nations based on its nonmember status *versus* validity of Article 2 (6) which empowers the United Nations to assume jurisdiction in the limited areas of international peace and security, and finally, (3) the PRC's general defiance, condemnation and rejection of the United Nations as a "tool of imperialism."

PRC's Claim of Self-Defense in Korea [6]

It must be recalled that under the principle of the United Nations Charter, self-defense as outlined in Article 51 of the Charter is the only exception to the general condemnation for the use of force (other than in actions under the auspices of the Organization.)

Even under the dictates of Article 51, individual usage of force is allowed only in rare and extraordinary cases wherein there exists an immediate danger to the sovereignty of a state resulting from illegal use of force by another state or states. Additionally, even in such cases, a state's action of "self-defense" is subject to Security Council inquiry and determination. In short, therefore, the right of "self-defense" is seemingly meant as a temporary right, to be exercised until the Security Council assumes jurisdiction over the case. And employment of force in the conduct of interstate relations is condemned once and for all, except in the

[6] For a discussion on the legal aspect of self-defense, see F. S. Lin, "Self-Defense—A Permissible Use of Force Under the U.N. Charter," *De Paul Law Review*, vol. 13 (1963), pp. 43-72; Marjorie M. Whiteman, *Digest of International Law*, vol. 10, pp. 1-27; Charles G. Fenwick, *International Law*, 4th ed., (New York: Appleton-Century-Crofts, 1965), pp. 271-295; William L. Tung, *International Law in an Organizing World*, (New York: Thomas Y. Crowell Co., 1968), pp. 131-132, 416-420; "Aggression, War, and Neutrality under the United Nations Charter," (A panel proceeding), *Proceedings of the American Society of International Law*, 1968, pp. 58-83.

circumstances of exceptional and immediate danger and only when resort to peaceful settlement is impossible, whatever the reason, without substantial expense to the sovereignty of the state.

In this connection, the foundation of Article 51 presumes existence of "external aggression," the definition of which is still lacking. Hence, other than in those cases which are determined as "aggressions," (under Article 39 of the Charter by the Security Council), there is no agreement on the type or nature of activities which constitute an "aggression." The finding of the General Assembly that PRC is "engaged in aggression in Korea" does not, in this connection, prejudice the right of the Council to make authoritative determination of "threat to the peace, breach of the peace, or act of aggression." It is, unfortunately, the inability of the Council to undertake such determination, whatever the reason, that caused the Assembly to assume the right to declare the PRC actions in Korea as an "aggression."

Other than the most apparent activities of "aggression" (such as invasion by armed forces, bombardment by naval and air forces, and the like) the essence of the problem in defining aggression centers around: (1) defining the initiator of aggression and its purpose; (2) the changing and changed nature in the means of aggression in recent years, due principally to advancements in weapons technology; and (3) difficulties inherent in overt as well as covert means of aggression in contemporary inter-state relations. Hence, the determination of *intent* and *activities* which constitute an "act of aggression" raises difficulties of insurmountable magnitude at least at the present juncture of international politics.

Several questions will illustrate the apparent difficulties in this connection: (1) Was an attack *intentionally* waged by the sponsor state for the *purpose* of committing aggression? This question involves objective *versus* subjective judgement of a given activity and the determination of which party or parties *in fact* and *in law* initiated the conflict. Related, of course, is (2) What kind of activity carried out in what manner constitutes an aggression?

While the established fact of military preparation for the exclusive purpose of waging aggressive war on a state may be a possible ground for certain defensive measures by the threatened state, it appears that the immediacy of the danger must be "overwhelming" before resort to force under the self-defense provision of Article 51 can be invoked. Given the present level of sophistication in military weaponry, it is doubtful that one can clearly distinguish between offensive and defensive military activities; nor will the immediacy of the danger necessarily be felt in the same degree by all states.

The "clear and present" danger concept and counter-measures "proportionate" to the threat posed know no agreed norms; additionally, given a use of force in a conflict, and given reciprocal allegations of "defensive" response by the belligerent states, the determination of those activities which constitute aggression (while it is a necessary precondition for the determination of "wrongdoers") is seemingly beyond the reach of contemporary global agreement.

The Soviet Union and the communist bloc nations have been insisting rather consistently that the right of "self-defense" under Article 51 should be limited to actual, direct, and clear cases of armed attack, and that the same right should not be entertained in any other case, even in the case of threat or use of force. The Western version, which appears to enjoy the support of the majority of the states in the United Nations, tends to take a broad and flexible definition of the right under Article 51. In short, the Western version seems to entertain the right of "self-defense" not only where a direct and clear case of armed attack exists but also in certain indirect instances of aggression which pose threat or use of force. While therefore the existence or lack of the rights under Article 51 is seemingly dependent upon the qualitative seriousness of the danger to the sovereignty of the victim state, it appears that determination of the point at which a given act of affront endows the right of self-defense seems near impossibility.

In the specific instance of Chinese "aggression" in Korea, Article 51 cannot be relied upon as its legal recourse; furthermore, the Security Council regarded it as being anything but a lawful, therefore defensive, action. And, ironically, as stated previously, under the Soviet version of rights of "self-defense," threat of aggression in the absence of actual armed attack cannot raise armed "self-defense," hence, the Chinese claim, if it is justified under Article 51, cannot be supported by the Soviet definition of Article 51.

PRC's Claim of Immunity

In view of the more detailed discussion on the problem of nonmember status elsewhere (Chapter II), only a general observation will be made here.

From the very outset, it is recalled that the nonmember status of PRC at that time did not preclude the United Nations from assuming jurisdiction in matters which are necessary or related to the organization's efforts to maintain international peace and security; the PRC's action in Korea during the war was, without a doubt, clearly a matter of grave importance to international peace and security. In short, the right of the United Nations to undertake actions in Korea and, in the course of which, to deal with PRC—insofar as its actions are related to international peace and security—seems unquestionable.

Again, in the standard of international community applicable then as is now, no state, irrespective of its membership status with the United Nations, may exempt its behaviour from the United Nations standard so long as its behavior is judged as related to the maintenance of international peace and security. Open belligerency and denial of United Nations competency by reason of its non-involvement and nonmember status does not appear plausible.

In the similar sense, to the extent that the Charter is an acknowledged norm of international relations and to the extent that Article 2 (6) is recognized as a necessary and valid claim to jurisdiction by the United Nations, as acknowledged by the overwhelming majority of nations in the world, PRC's claim of immunity has to be judged as baseless and any actions undertaken in that guise which violate the Charter must be judged as defiance.

PRC's Defiance, Condemnation and Rejection of the United Nations

As for the PRC's defiance to discuss in the United Nations its role in the Korean war or to settle the issue through peaceful means in accordance with the dictates of the United Nations, or its rejection of the United Nations' right of involvement in the conflict, or, so far as that goes, its denial of the very basis of the United Nations, they are totally beyond the realm of contemporary international law. The question is not so much one of belligerency in the Korean war in support of North Korea but one of belligerent defiance to the very foundation of the United Nations.

As had been observed earlier, PRC had been consistent in denying the United Nations as a competent international machinery charged with undertaking certain actions; indeed, claims have been made that the United Nations is merely a forum for legitimatizing the exploitation of colonial people by the capitalists. Needless to say, and not withstanding PRC's membership status presently, this is a defiance of a very serious nature; for in all possible accounts of investigation and analysis, and unless it can be maintained that the Charter and the actions undertaken in accordance with it are in violation of international law, denial of the United Nations as a competent organ to deal with problems of war and peace is indeed to deny the validity of an international standard because of its conflict with a state's interest, however arrived.

Nor should this fundamental denial of validity of the United Nations be regarded as merely a matter of "whose international law" one is utilizing at a time. Defiant activities of a state against international norms are only subject to the three conditions cited earlier; that is, defiance and defiant activities are so regarded provided that: (1) prevalent international politics does not significantly alter the standard; (2) subsequent action of the organization does not, either explicitly or implicitly, change the defiant status, (3) the decision-making majority in the organization remains substantially the same in composition.

Yet, the claim to jurisdiction and ability to exercise actual control over the matters so claimed should have a reasonably close relationship. When there is no such relationship the organization is losing its real power and influence, due to the loss of confidence, and thereby encouraging further avoidance, noncompliance or defiance by its members and nonmembers.

It appears safe, therefore, to assert that the advantages of flexibility stemming from pragmatically arrived decisions should be measured in consideration of the disadvantages of being misconstrued as having no standard at all in international relations.

CHAPTER XI

APPRAISAL

An international organization is never an end in itself; it exists to serve common interests of its members. Furthermore, because an international organization is not a world government, it is even more dependent upon the willing support of the membership for its viability than is a municipal government.

Fluidity of international politics negates the establishment of absolute international standards; yet, the United Nations symbolizes an effort to establish guidelines for a better world. A recent assessment of the organization's first quarter century concludes that "the United Nations continues to justify its existence in many fields of activity for the promotion of human welfare and of a spirit of community, however short it has come of the role once envisaged for it as a legal authority sufficiently adequate for keeping the peace." [1] At this critical point in world affairs, it would be next to impossible to devise an alternative to its ideals with better prospects of success. This is so, not only because human capacity for creating tomorrow's world is marred by today's problems but also because the source of ineffectiveness in the United Nations is less a matter of its constitutional structure and functions than it is a contradiction between the tasks which the collective membership assigns the organization and the willingness of states individually affected by these decisions to accept them. The contradiction is more notable because it highlights the organization's inadequate power to implement its decisions and thereby threatens its prestige and effectiveness. This contradiction is heightened by the quantity and quality of new international obligations and the diversity of membership in the United Nations.

[1] Robert R. Wilson "The United Nations as Symbol and As Instrument," *American Journal of International Law*, vol. 64 (1970), p. 143.

Irrespective of size, power or stage of development, all United Nations members have contributed to these contradictions. The evolution of the Charter was begun by the original members and it has been continued in the same general direction as new states have been admitted. Some members may have acted more cynically than others, but all have exhibited a tendency to support a wide range of international actions that do not immediately and directly affect them and a zealous protectionism of their own direct or immediate interests. Nonmembers are not immune from this charge; no particular category of states appears most guilty; nor is the phenomemon peculiar to this decade or century.

The limited selection of cases that has been included here may suggest that the big and medium powers have relied more on the techniques of avoidance or noncompliance than the small powers, or that defiant activities are more often utilized by small and medium powers, but a broader sampling suggests no such pattern. Consider, for example, such major power actions as United States justifications of quarantine during the Cuban crisis, the Bay of Pigs invasion, or its participation in the Vietnam War. To include both sides in the cold war, consider the Soviet Union's involvement in Hungary (1956) and Czechoslovakia (1968) and its justification of the refusal to pay certain expenses associated with the operations in the Middle East and the Congo. Certainly, these are not consistent with the ideals of the United Nations for a better world founded on peace and harmony. It may be that both states have justified their actions on various legal and political grounds, but the contradiction between promises as members of the United Nations and performance when confronted with matters of immediate and specific interests are beyond question.

As United Nations membership has increased, the magnitude of this contradiction has increased and its focus has been affected by the developing states. The initial membership of fifty-one has almost tripled. A majority in 1945 that had a western orientation has been transformed into one that is non-western. Many of the current members have been former colonies or protectorates of some of the founding nations. Accordingly, the general tone and spirit of the organization tend to reflect not only the flavor of newly independent Afro-Asian nations but also their fervor to use the United Nations as an instrument for attaining goals which appear to be beyond its practical reach, or are beyond the willingness of individual states to comply. Many of the problems which the United Nations is asked to settle relate very closely to the dilemmas of these developing nations. As illustrated by the Congo crisis, internal divisions of these new states increase international pressures which their nationalism leads them to resist.

Any consideration of the capacity of states to succeed in techniques of avoidance, noncompliance or defiance must include the observation that the major and medium powers are better equipped to succeed in recalcitrant acts than are the developing nations. The major powers have the veto in Security Council deliberations and the resources to mount an enormous campaign to influence votes in all organs. Major power efforts at self-protection by trading support to avoid obligations and the dimensions of the cold war assure that whatever side a state chooses in a given contest, it almost invariably has ready support from a big power. And so long as the cold war foreshadows any juridical approach to the problem of resolving international disputes, states are likely to continue avoidance, noncompliance, or defiance to international norms. It was this firm support of a major power that enabled the new government in Czechoslovakia to avoid international interference in 1948. Although the cold war entered into the Congo crisis, it was probably the absence of a firm commitment from either side in the great power struggle that enabled the United Nations to disregard the objections of the Congolese government.

In evaluating the trends in international commitments one recalls the observation made in 1960 by Professor Oscar Schachter [2] that, while the record of compliance with international decisions by member states is good, it could deteriorate as more states achieve full partnership in the international community and as international organs attempt to deal with more issues and problems of greater import to member states. Indeed, the span of a decade has brought about changes not only in the quantity of problems over which jurisdiction is claimed by the United Nations but also in the quality of issues having greater significance to member states. Consider, for example, the magnitude or the international obligations that could result from a major international effort to resolve environmental problems.

In the final analysis, an international organization relies upon the consent and support of its members and its members join the international arrangements for their national interests. Although the basic interests of international organizations and member states should not be in contra-

[2] Oscar Schachter, "Enforcement of International Judicial and Arbitral Decisions," *American Journal of International Law*, vol. 54 (1960), pp. 1-24.

diction, they have the potential for conflict that has been a theme of this study. Consequently, an international organization and its members must be ever mindful of the problems arising from conflicts. The assessment of obligations to international organizations and the related examinations contained in this volume are merely illustrations of efforts of the world community to balance the need of international peace and security against the desires of states to manage their own affairs.

The equilibrium between the jurisdictions of states and the international organization depends on the original constitutive document. In a changing world, this document must be adaptable to the needs of the time. Yet, an international organization must avoid overtaxing its real capabilities; that is to say, the principle of balance between prerogatives of member states (and nonmember states, as well) and that of the international organization must be maintained.

A significant over-extension in the equilibrium in favor of the international organization will damage the latter because of its lack of independently available force. Conversely, significant state successes in disregarding international organization norms will decrease the power and prestige of the international organization, hence making it meaningless. Herein lies the challenge to scholars and practitioners of international relations. They must assess the political realities of the international situation in order to maintain this balance.

At this time, it appears reasonable to assert that an international organization such as the United Nations will not for long remain a significant force for world order and international peace if: (1) one or more of the major powers continues to avoid obligations or to resort to defiance, or (2) even assuming major power support, a significant number of medium and small states decide collectively to undertake similar acts, or (3) there be continued avoidances, noncompliances and defiances which are left unanswered over a long period of time, or (4) the organization substantially exceeds and over-extends its functions beyond its *real* capacity.

The experience of the League of Nations stands as a vivid reminder that continued and unanswered defiance of Covenant obligations ultimately led to its unfortunate demise. The United Nations has weathered more than twenty-five formative years, but the coming quarter-century threatens to be more difficult than the last. If the organization is to remain viable, serious consideration must be given to these threats to its survival.

INDEX

GPSR Compliance

The European Union's (EU) General Product Safety Regulation (GPSR) is a set of rules that requires consumer products to be safe and our obligations to ensure this.

If you have any concerns about our products, you can contact us on ProductSafety@springernature.com

In case Publisher is established outside the EU, the EU authorized representative is:

Springer Nature Customer Service Center GmbH
Europaplatz 3
69115 Heidelberg, Germany

Batch number: 10830943

Printed by Printforce, the Netherlands